MW01091934

STATE V. GRAY

STATE V. GRAY

A. J. Bellido de Luna

University of Maryland
Francis King Carey School of Law

Joseph E. Taylor

University of the Pacific
McGeorge School of Law

NATIONAL INSTITUTE FOR TRIAL ADVOCACY

© 2016 by the National Institute for Trial Advocacy

All rights reserved. No part of this work may be reproduced or transmitted in any form or by any means, electronic or mechanical, including photocopying and recording, or by any information storage or retrieval system without the prior written approval of the National Institute for Trial Advocacy unless such copying is expressly permitted by federal copyright law.

Law students who purchase this NITA publication as part of their class materials and attendees of NITA-sponsored CLE programs are granted a limited license to reproduce, enlarge, and electronically or physically display, in their classrooms or other educational settings, any exhibits or text contained in all formats of the publication whether printed or electronic. However, sharing one legally purchased copy of the publication among several members of a class team is prohibited under this license. Each individual is required to purchase his or her own copy of this publication. See 17 U.S.C. § 106.

Address inquiries to:

Reprint Permission
National Institute for Trial Advocacy
1685 38th Street, Suite 200
Boulder, CO 80301-2735
Phone: (800) 225-6482
Fax: (720) 890-7069
Email: permissions@nita.org

ISBN 978-1-06156-613-3
eISBN 978-1-60156-614-0
FBA 1613

Printed in the United States of America

CONTENTS

Acknowledgments

The authors would like to acknowledge the special contributions to the development of this case file made by Bobby Carlson, Esq. and Amanda Sentele, Esq., former students of the University of Maryland Francis King Carey School of Law.

We also want to extend our appreciation to the public media including the CNN Network for obtaining and making available to the public original evidence in the recent Ferguson and Baltimore cases.

Readers of this case file should know and understand that it does not mirror the two cases mentioned above, and efforts have been made to balance this case file and fictionalize much of the content.

Thanks also to the 1947 Boston Red Sox baseball team for providing the names of all characters in this *State v. Gray* case file.

AUTHORS' NOTE

The events occurring in Ferguson during the summer of 2014, in Baltimore and Chicago in 2015, and other similar events throughout our nation have energized the country in a debate about police tactics in America. If we are to move forward as a nation, then having open discussions about these topics is important. The issue in this case file is the use of force and whether the shooting of an unarmed individual was appropriate and justified. The issue of race is purposely deleted. This is so because a user may wish to avoid the race issue and deal only with whether the shooting of an unarmed individual is justified based on law. Nita City and Darrow County, which are fictional, were used for this problem.

This statement is not part of the case to be tried and may not be used by either party during the course of the trial.

INTRODUCTION

On August 9, YR-1, eighteen-year-old Rudy York was walking with his friend Johnny Pesky on the travel portion of the roadway of Cranfield Drive, in Nita City, Darrow County, in the State of Nita. Cranfield Drive is a two-lane, southeast–northwest residential street with sidewalks on both sides of the street. Officer Darren Gray was patrolling the same neighborhood and saw York and Pesky walking in the roadway. Officer Gray drove up and from inside of his patrol car, he told them to get out of the street. A few moments later, York was shot by Officer Gray and York died at the scene. An autopsy was performed on August 17, YR-1, showing that York died from the gunshot wounds and that he was shot nine times by Officer Gray. All nine shots were fired while York was facing Officer Gray. York was unarmed.

Prosecution Case

The prosecution witness Johnny Pesky contends there was no traffic and that suddenly Officer Gray drove up and yelled to get off the street. They did, and Officer Gray pulled up next to them, blocked them from moving, and grabbed York. Officer Gray then choked him, pulled out his gun and threatened to shoot him. Gray then fired a shot, hitting York. Pesky and York ran away, and Officer Gray ran after them. York was shot a second time, and he put his hands in the air. Officer Gray fired several more shots, killing York. The crime scene technician's examination concluded Officer Gray's car did not have any fingerprints from York and that the only place York's DNA could be found was on the driver's door panel. Prosecution expert witness Captain Tebbetts concluded that Officer Gray used force greater than necessary under the case facts, in violation of law enforcement standards and protocols.

Defense Case

Officer Gray described the events of that day. He said that around noon he was on duty, in full uniform in a police car, and was responding to a call about a sick baby when he saw Rudy York and Johnny Pesky walking down the middle of the street, causing cars to slow down and drive around them. He stopped near them and asked them to walk on the sidewalk. York walked up to his window and swore at him, and they continued walking down the street. Officer Gray drove close to them, blocking their path, and had opened his door when York swore at him again and slammed his patrol car door. York stood next to the driver's door, Officer Gray pushed his door open, and York slammed it shut and hit Officer Gray with his fist. Officer Gray tried to get out of the car and York hit him again. Officer Gray then pulled his gun and told York to get back or he would shoot him. York grabbed the gun and swore at him, and Officer Gray felt York's hand on the gun, Officer Gray pulled it away, and the gun fired. York backed up, and then came back to Officer Gray with his hands up and struck Officer Gray again. Officer Gray pulled the trigger, it clicked once, and he fired twice while Officer Gray was in the car and York ran off.

Officer Gray got out of the car and chased York. York stopped, turned around, glared at Officer Grey, and ran toward him with his fist cocked and his other hand under his shirt. Officer Gray told him several times to get on the ground, but York kept running toward him. Officer Gray backed up and fired off several shots, and York continued running toward him. Officer Gray backed up further and told York to get on the ground. He was eight to ten feet from York, who continued to run at him. Officer Gray fired at York's head and York fell to the ground.

Throughout the process, Officer Gray feared for his life and fired his weapon only when he was in fear of his own life. He felt that York may have had a weapon in his hand under his shirt. Officer Gray suffered injuries from the punches to his head. His face was swollen on both his right and left cheeks, he had red marks and scratches on his neck and the hairline, and he received medical treatment.

SPECIAL INSTRUCTIONS FOR USE AS A FULL TRIAL

When this case file is used for a full trial, each party is limited to calling the following witnesses:

State of Nita   Johnny Pesky

Detective Sergeant Billy Goodman

Captain Birdie Tebbetts

Whitney Moses

Defendant   Officer Darren Gray

Denny Galehouse

Dr. Mel Parnell

Dr. Rousey Williams ✗

Discovery Obligations

Pursuant to Nita Criminal Code § 1054.3, which requires the defense to disclose names, addresses, relevant written statements, and reports of witnesses the defense intends to call at trial, the reports and statements of defense witnesses Denny Galehouse, Dr. Mel Parnell, and Dr. Rousey Williams have been disclosed to the prosecution.

Pursuant to Nita Criminal Code § 1054.2, Nita City Police Department case reports were disclosed to the defense by the prosecution.

Required Stipulations

1)   The defendant Darren Gray and the witness Johnny Pesky are male. All other witnesses may be either male or female.

2)   The autopsy report and body diagram of Dr. Louis Bader dated August 19, YR-1, are admissible as evidence. Counsel will stipulate to the qualifications of Dr. Bader to render an expert opinion as to the results of that autopsy examination.

Pretrial Motions

The defendant moved to suppress all statements he made to Nita City Police Department Detective Sergeant Billy Goodman on Fifth, Sixth, and Fourteenth Amendment grounds. The court ruled these statements were admissible.

The prosecution moved to suppress any statements that Johnny Pesky made to Detective Sergeant Billy Goodman in the initial interview on August 12, YR-1, on grounds that Pesky was interviewed under involuntary circumstances when he was made to believe that he could be prosecuted unless he helped prove that Officer Gray was the victim, thus denying Pesky his Fifth, Sixth, and Fourteenth Amendment rights. The court denied that motion.

Additionally, the prosecution moved to exclude any testimony by defense expert Dr. Rousey Williams of previous cases at which both Captain Tebbetts and Dr. Williams appeared and gave testimony in and the results of the those trials. The court declined to rule on those issues until the court hears more specific information from both counsel.

The legal issues that the court has ruled on may not be re-litigated at trial.

All years in these materials are stated in the following form:

- YR-0 indicates the actual year in which the case is being tried (i.e., the present year);

- YR-1 indicates the next preceding year (please use the actual year);

- YR-2 indicates the second preceding year (please use the actual year), etc.

Electronic versions of the exhibits are available for download here:

http://bit.ly/1P20Jea

Password: Gray1

**IN THE DISTRICT COURT
OF THE STATE OF NITA
COUNTY OF DARROW**

THE STATE OF NITA   )
)   Case No. CR 3914-YR-1
v.   )
)   INFORMATION
DARREN GRAY,   )
Defendant.   )

THE STATE OF NITA does hereby charge that the defendant, DARREN GRAY, on 9th day of August, YR-1, at and within the County of Darrow, did commit the crime of murder of the second degree, a felony, in violation of Section 102 of the Criminal Code of the State of Nita, in that he did knowingly, willfully, feloniously, and intentionally, but not after deliberation, cause the death of Rudy York, a human being, contrary to the form, force, and effect of the law of the State of Nita and against the peace and dignity of the People of the State of Nita.

DATED: September 11, YR-1

Carol Palica
_____

Alexander Haugstad, District Attorney
by Carol Palica, Deputy District Attorney
County of Darrow, State of Nita

Charge
_____
Murder 2ⁿᵈ degree

EXHIBITS

Map of Shooting Scene

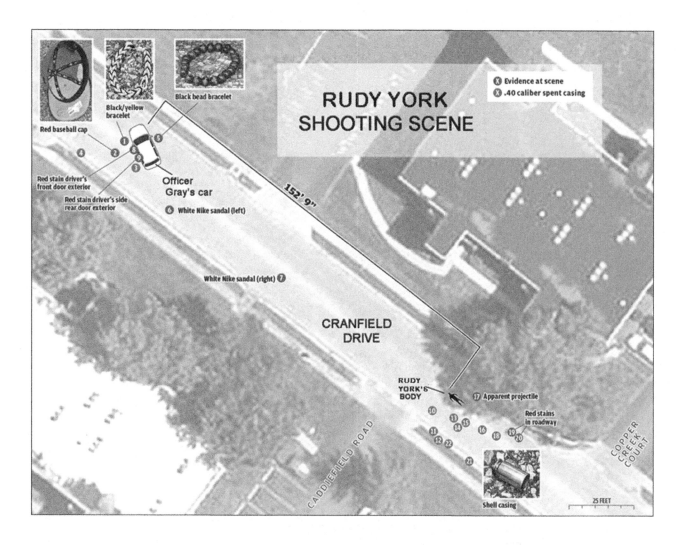

you will see
a map of the
shooting scene
- photos of the
police car, the
body, the weapon
protests,

Exhibit 2

Photo of Officer Gray's Vehicle

Exhibit 3

Photo of Officer Gray's Vehicle Driver's Door Open

Exhibit 4

Photo of Body

Exhibit 5

Photo of Officer Gray's Gun

Exhibit 6

Photo of Protests

Exhibit 7

**Nita City Police Manual:
Section 8.0, Use of Force**

USE OF FORCE—CORE PRINCIPLES

1) **Every member of the Nita City Police Department is committed to upholding the Constitution and laws of the United States and the State of Nita, and defending the civil rights and dignity of all individuals, while protecting human life and property and maintaining civil order.**

It is the policy of the Nita City Police Department to accomplish the police mission with the cooperation of the public and as effectively as possible, and with minimal reliance upon the use of physical force.

The community expects, and the Nita City Police Department requires, that officers use only the force necessary to perform their duties and that such force be proportional to the threat or resistance of the subject under the circumstances.

An officer's commitment to public safety includes the welfare of members of the public, the officer, and fellow officers, with an emphasis on respect, professionalism, and protection of human life, even when force is necessary.

Officers who violate those values by using objectively unreasonable force degrade the confidence of the community, violate the rights of individuals upon whom unreasonable force is used, and may expose the department and fellow officers to legal and physical hazards.

Conversely, officers who fail to use timely and adequate force when it is necessary fail in their duty to act as public guardians, and may endanger themselves, the community, and fellow officers.

2) **When time, circumstances, and safety permit, officers will take steps to gain compliance and de-escalate conflict without using physical force.**

When safe under the totality of circumstances, and time and circumstances permit, officers shall use advisements, warnings, verbal persuasion, and other tactics in order to reduce the need to use force.

Officers should consider whether a subject's lack of compliance is a deliberate attempt to resist or an inability to comply based on factors including, but not limited to:

- Medical conditions

- Mental impairment

- Developmental disability

- Physical limitation

- Language barrier

- Drug interaction

- Behavioral crisis

3) **Sometimes the use of force is unavoidable and an officer must exercise physical control of a violent assaultive, or resisting, individual to make an arrest, or to protect members of the public or officers from risk of harm.**

    In doing so:

    - Officers should recognize that their conduct prior to the use of force, including the display of a weapon, may be a factor which can influence the level of force necessary in a given situation.

    - Officers should take reasonable care not to place themselves or others in jeopardy, or fail to follow policy or training, so that their actions do not precipitate an unnecessary, unreasonable, or disproportionate use of force.

    - Officers should continually assess the situation and changing circumstances, and modulate the use of force appropriately

4) **An officer shall use only the degree of force that is objectively reasonable, necessary under the circumstances, and proportional to the threat or resistance of a subject.**

    Objectively reasonable. The reasonableness of a particular use of force is based on the totality of circumstances known by the officer at the time of the use of force. It weighs the actions of the officer against the rights of the subject, in light of the circumstances surrounding the event. It must be judged from the perspective of a reasonable officer on the scene, rather than with the 20/20 vision of hindsight.

    The calculus of reasonableness must embody allowance for the fact that police officers are often forced to make split-second decisions—in circumstances that are tense, uncertain, and rapidly evolving—about the amount of force that is necessary in a particular situation.

The reasonableness inquiry in an excessive-force case is an objective one: the question is whether the officers' actions are objectively reasonable in light of the facts and circumstances confronting them, without regard to their underlying intent or motivation.

Necessary. Officers will use physical force only when no reasonably effective alternative appears to exist, and only then to the degree that is reasonable to effect a lawful purpose.

Proportional. The level of force applied must reflect the totality of circumstances surrounding the situation, including the presence of imminent danger to officers or others. Proportional force does not require officers to use the same type or amount of force as the subject. The more immediate the threat and the more likely that the threat will result in death or serious physical injury, the greater the level of force that may be objectively reasonable and necessary to counter it.

5) **Each officer is responsible for explaining and articulating the specific facts, and reasonable inferences from those facts, that justify the officer's use of force.**

The officer's justification will be reviewed to determine whether the force used was in or out of policy. Failure to adequately document and explain the facts, circumstances, and inferences when reporting force may lead to the conclusion that the force used was out of policy.

6) **The department is committed to upholding lawful, professional, and ethical standards through assertive leadership and supervision before, during, and after every force incident.**

The Nita City Police Department recognizes the magnitude of the responsibility that comes with the constitutional authority to use force. This responsibility includes maintaining vigorous standards and transparent oversight systems to ensure accountability to the community to maintain its trust. This includes:

- Force prevention efforts,
- Effective tactics, and
- Objective review and analysis of all incidents of reportable force

7) **A strong partnership between the department and the community is essential for effective enforcement and public safety.**

Uses of force, even if lawful and proper, can have a damaging effect on the public's perception of the department and the department's relationship with the community.

Both the department and individual officers need to be aware of the negative effects of use-of-force incidents and be empowered to take appropriate action to mitigate these effects, such as:

- Explaining actions to subjects or members of the public

- Offering reasonable aid to those affected by a use-of-force

- Treating subjects, witnesses, and bystanders with professionalism and courtesy

- Department follow-up with neighbors or family to explain police actions and hear concerns and feedback

USE OF FORCE—DEFINITIONS

Deadly Force. The application of force through the use of firearms or any other means reasonably likely to cause death, great bodily harm, or serious physical injury.

When reasonably likely to cause death or serious physical injury, deadly force includes:

- Shooting a firearm at a person

- A hard strike to a person's head, neck, or throat with an impact weapon

- Striking a person's head into a hard, fixed object. Examples include, but are not limited to:

  ▪ Street surfaces

  ▪ Solid metal structures, such as bars or guardrails

  ▪ Shooting a person in the head or neck with a beanbag shotgun round

  ▪ Using stop-sticks on a moving motorcycle

- Neck and carotid restraints may only be used when deadly force is authorized.

De-escalation. Taking action to stabilize the situation and reduce the immediacy of the threat so that more time, options, and resources are available to resolve the situation. The goal of de-escalation is to gain voluntary compliance of subjects, when feasible, and reduce or eliminate the necessity to use physical force.

De-escalation techniques. Actions used by officers, when safe and without compromising law enforcement priorities, that seek to minimize the likelihood of the need to use force during an incident and increase the likelihood of gaining voluntary compliance from a subject.

Force. Force means any physical coercion by an officer in performance of official duties, including the following types of force.

- **De minimis force**. Physical interaction meant to separate, guide, and /or control without the use of control techniques that are intended to or are reasonably likely to cause any pain or injury. Includes:

- Use of control holds or joint manipulation techniques in a manner that does not cause any pain and is not reasonably likely to cause any pain.

- Using hands or equipment to stop, push back, separate, or escort a person without causing any pain or in a manner that would not reasonably cause any pain.

- **Type I.** Force that causes transitory pain, the complaint of transitory pain, disorientation, or the intentional pointing of a firearm or beanbag shotgun.

- **Type II.** Force that causes or is reasonably expected to cause physical injury greater than transitory pain but less than great or substantial bodily harm, and/or the use of any of the following weapons or instruments: conducted electrical weapon (CEW) (Taser), oleoresin capsicum (OC) spray, impact weapon, beanbag shotgun, deployment of K-9 with injury or complaint of injury causing less than Type III injury, vehicle, hobble restraint.

- **Type III.** Force that causes or is reasonably expected to cause great bodily harm, substantial bodily harm, loss of consciousness, or death, and/or the use of neck or carotid holds, stop-sticks for motorcycles, impact weapon strikes to the head.

Force Investigation Team (FIT). The department personnel tasked with conducting Officer-Involved Shootings and Type III use-of-force investigations.

Injury classifications. The following are classifications of injury used by the NCPD.

- **Physical or bodily injury** (also "Injury"). Physical pain or injury, illness, or an impairment of physical condition greater than transitory pain but less than great or substantial bodily harm.

- **Serious physical injury**. Physical injury that creates a substantial risk of death or causes serious disfigurement, serious impairment of health, or serious loss or impairment of the function of any bodily organ or structure, or involves serious concussive impact to the head.

- **Substantial bodily harm**. Bodily injury that involves:

  - Temporary but substantial disfigurement

  - Temporary but substantial loss or impairment of the function of any bodily part or organ

  - Fracture of any bodily part

- **Great bodily harm**. Bodily injury that:

  - Creates a probability of death

  - Causes significant, serious permanent disfigurement

- Causes a significant, permanent loss or impairment of the function of any bodily part or organ

Less lethal devices. Devices designed and intended to apply force for which the outcome is not intended nor likely to cause the death of the subject or great bodily harm. Includes Taser, impact weapons, beanbag shotgun, oleoresin capsicum (OC) spray.

Necessary force. "Necessary" means that no reasonably effective alternative to the use of force appeared to exist and that the amount of force used was reasonable to effect the lawful purpose intended.

Objectively reasonable force. Objectively reasonable force is based on the totality of circumstances known by the officer at the time of the use of force and weighs the actions of the officer against the rights of the subject, in light of the circumstances surrounding the event. It must be judged from the perspective of a reasonable officer at the scene rather than with the 20/20 vision of hindsight.

Reportable force. All uses of force other than de minimis are reportable. Reportable force includes the intentional pointing of a firearm at a subject.

Use of force. See **Force**.

Weapons.

- **Approved weapon**. A tool used to apply force that is both specified and authorized by the department.

- **Approved use of a weapon**. Use of an approved weapon by an officer who has been properly trained and certified in the use of that weapon.

- **Impact weapon**. Any authorized intermediate weapon or object used to strike a subject and inflict pain or injury through blunt force.

- **Improvised weapon**. An object used to apply force other than those approved and authorized by the department. Also, any department-approved weapon used by an officer who has not received required training or certification to use the weapon.

USE OF FORCE—USING FORCE

1) **Use of Force—When Authorized**

An officer shall use only the force reasonable, necessary, and proportionate to effectively bring an incident or person under control, while protecting the lives of the officer or others.

In other words, when necessary, officers shall only use objectively reasonable force, proportional to the threat or urgency of the situation to achieve a law enforcement objective.

The force used must comply with federal and state law and Nita City Police Department policies, training, and rules for specific instruments and devices. Once it is safe to do so and the threat is contained and/or the subject complies with the officer's orders, the force must stop. When determining if the force was objectively reasonable, necessary, and proportionate—and therefore authorized—the following guidelines will be applied.

Reasonable. The reasonableness of a particular use of force is based on the totality of circumstances known by the officer at the time of the use of force and weighs the actions of the officer against the rights of the subject, in light of the circumstances surrounding the event. It must be judged from the perspective of a reasonable officer on the scene rather than with the 20/20 vision of hindsight. Factors to be considered in determining the objective reasonableness of force include, but are not limited to:

- The seriousness of the crime or suspected offense

- The level of threat or resistance presented by the subject

- Whether the subject was posing an immediate threat to officers or a danger to the community

- The potential for injury to citizens, officers, or subjects

- The risk of, or apparent attempt by the subject to, escape

- The conduct of the subject being confronted (as reasonably perceived by the officer at the time)

- The time available to an officer to make a decision

- The availability of other resources

- The training and experience of the officer

- The proximity or access of weapons to the subject

- Officer versus subject factors such as age, size, relative strength, skill level, injury/exhaustion, and number of officers versus subjects

- The environmental factors and/or other exigent circumstances

The assessment of reasonableness must embody allowance for the fact that police officers are often forced to make split-second decisions—in circumstances that are tense, uncertain, and rapidly evolving—about the amount of force that is necessary in a particular situation.

The reasonableness inquiry in an excessive-force case is an objective one: the question is whether the officers' actions are objectively reasonable in light of the facts and circumstances confronting them, without regard to their underlying intent or motivation.

Necessary. Officers will use physical force only when no reasonably effective alternative appears to exist, and only then to the degree that is reasonable to effect a lawful purpose.

Proportional. To be proportional, the level of force applied must reflect the totality of circumstances surrounding the immediate situation, including the presence of an imminent danger to officers or others. Officers must rely on training, experience, and assessment of the situation to decide an appropriate level of force to be applied. Reasonable and sound judgment will dictate the force option to be employed. Proportional force does not require officers to use the same type or amount of force as the subject. The more immediate the threat and the more likely that the threat will result in death or serious physical injury, the greater the level of force that may be proportional, objectively reasonable, and necessary to counter it.

2) **Use of force: when prohibited.**

An officer may not use physical force:

- To punish or retaliate

- Against individuals who only confront them unless vocalization impedes a legitimate law enforcement function or contains specific threats to harm the officers or others

- On handcuffed or otherwise restrained subjects except in exceptional circumstances when the subject's actions must be immediately stopped to prevent injury, escape, or destruction of property. Use-of-force on restrained subjects shall be closely and critically reviewed. Officers must articulate both:

  - The exceptional circumstances *and*

  - Why no reasonably effective alternative to the use-of-force appeared to exist

- To stop a subject from swallowing a substance, such as a plastic bag containing a controlled substance or other evidence

- To extract a substance or item from inside the body of a suspect without a warrant

3) **When safe under the totality of the circumstances and time and when circumstances permit, officers shall use de-escalation tactics to reduce the need for force.**

De-escalation tactics and techniques are actions used by officers, when safe and without compromising law enforcement priorities, that seek to minimize the likelihood of the need to use force during an incident.

When safe and feasible under the totality of circumstances, officers shall attempt to slow down or stabilize the situation so that more time, options, and resources are available for incident resolution.

When time and circumstances reasonably permit, officers shall consider whether a subject's lack of compliance is a deliberate attempt to resist or an inability to comply based on factors including, but not limited to:

- Medical conditions

- Mental impairment

- Developmental disability

- Physical imitation

- Language barrier

- Drug interaction

- Behavioral crisis

An officer's awareness of these possibilities, when time and circumstances reasonably permit, shall then be balanced against the facts of the incident when deciding which tactical options are the most appropriate to bring the situation to a safe resolution.

Mitigating the immediacy of threat gives officers time to utilize extra resources and increases time available to call more officers or specialty units.

The number of officers on scene may increase the available force options and may increase the ability to reduce the overall force used.

Other examples include:

- Placing barriers between an uncooperative subject and an officer

- Containing a threat

- Moving from a position that exposes officers to potential threats to a safer position

- Decreasing the exposure to potential threat by using:

  - Distance

  - Cover

  - Concealment

- Communication, from a safe position, intended to gain the subject's compliance by using:

  - Verbal persuasion

- Advisements

- Warnings

- Avoidance of physical confrontation, unless immediately necessary (for example, to protect someone or stop dangerous behavior)

- Using verbal techniques, such as Listen and Explain with Equity and Dignity (LEED) Training, to calm an agitated subject and promote rational decision making

- Calling extra resources to assist or officers to assist:

  - More officers

  - Crisis intervention team (CIT) officers

  - Officers equipped with less-lethal tools

- Any other tactics and approaches that attempt to achieve law enforcement objectives by gaining the compliance of the subject

4) **Officers should assess and modulate the use-of-force as resistance decreases.**

For example, as resistance decreases, the use of force may decrease.

5) **Use of deadly force.**

Deadly force may only be used in circumstances where threat of death or serious physical injury to the officer or others is imminent. A danger is imminent when an objectively reasonable officer would conclude that:

- A suspect is acting or threatening to cause death or serious physical injury to the officer or others, and

- The suspect has the means or instrumentalities to do so, and

- The suspect has the opportunity and ability to use the means or instrumentalities to cause death or serious physical injury

6) **Deadly force may be used to prevent the escape of a fleeing suspect only when an objectively reasonable officer would conclude that it is necessary and the officer has probable cause to believe that:**

- The suspect has committed a felony involving the infliction or threatened infliction of serious physical injury or death, and

- The escape of the suspect would pose an imminent danger of death or serious physical injury to the officer or to another person unless the suspect is apprehended without delay, and

- The officer has given a verbal warning to the suspect, if time, safety, and circumstances permit

7) **Following a use-of-force, officers shall render or request medical aid, if needed or if requested by anyone, as soon as reasonably possible.**

Following a use of force, officers will request a medical aid response, if necessary, for suspects and others and will closely monitor subjects taken into custody.

Absent exigent circumstances, prone subjects will be placed on their side in a recover position. Officers shall not restrain subjects who are in custody and under control in a manner that compromises the subject's ability to breathe.

8) **Officers shall automatically request medical aid in certain situations.**

Any use of force greater than de minimis force on subjects who are reasonably believed or known to be:

- Pregnant

- Pre-adolescent children

- Elderly

- Physically frail

Any subjects or officers who:

- Sustain a conducted electrical weapon (CEW) (Taser) application

- Are struck by a beanbag shotgun round

- Sustain an impact weapon strike to the head

- Sustain a strike of their head against a hard, fixed object

9) **Consistent with timelines (noted in 8.3), officers and supervisors shall ensure that the incident is accurately and properly reported, documented, and investigated.**

USE OF FORCE—TOOLS

This policy addresses the use and deployment of all force tools that are available to sworn department employees.

The following force options are governed by this policy:

- Beanbag shotgun
- Canine deployment
- Conducted electrical weapons (CEW) (Taser)
- Firearms
- Impact weapons
- Oleoresin capsicum (OC) spray
- Vehicle-related force tactics
- Specialty unit weaponry
- Hobble restraint
- Neck and carotid restraint

The Intended Purpose of Less Lethal Devices

Less lethal devices are used to interrupt a subject's threatening behavior so that officers may take physical control of the subject with less risk of injury to the subject or officer than posed by greater force applications. Less lethal devices alone cannot be expected to render all suspects harmless.

Support officers should be prepared to take immediate action, if necessary, to exploit the brief opportunity created by the less-lethal device and take control of the subject if safe to do so.

1) **Officers will only carry and use weapons that have been approved by the department and that the officer has been properly trained and certified to use, except under exigent circumstances.**

   Intentional or reckless violations of policy or training standards will result in discipline. Negligent violations of policy or training standards may result in discipline.

2) **Uniformed officers are required to carry at least one less lethal tool.**

   Uniformed officers who have been issued a conducted electrical weapon (CEW) shall carry it.

3) **Sergeants and lieutenants will ensure that each officer in their command is trained and certified on the tools they carry, as required.**

4) **Officers are prohibited from using less lethal tools as a form of punishment or for retaliation.**

5) **Officers are prohibited from using less lethal tools or other techniques in the following circumstances, absent active aggression by the suspect that cannot be reasonably dealt with in any other fashion.**

- When the suspect is visibly pregnant, elderly, preadolescent, visibly frail, or known or suspected to be disabled, unless deadly force is the only other option

- When the suspect is in an elevated position where a fall is likely to cause substantial injury or death

- When the suspect is in a location where the suspect could drown

- When the suspect is operating a motor vehicle or motorcycle and the engine is running or is on a bicycle or scooter in motion

- When an individual is handcuffed or otherwise restrained

- To escort, prod, or jab individuals

- To awaken unconscious or intoxicated individuals

- To prevent the destruction of evidence

- Against passive or low-level resisting subjects

- When the suspect is detained in the police vehicle

BEANBAG SHOTGUN

A beanbag shotgun is designed to temporarily interrupt the behavior of a suspect or dangerous individual so that law enforcement officers can subdue and arrest that person with less danger of injury or death to themselves and others.

1) **Firearms Training Squad (FTS) manages the beanbag shotgun program.**

FTS will maintain the beanbag shotgun operator's manual, develop curriculum, and conduct training and qualifications.

2) **FTS will train and certify operators annually.**

Only officers who have been trained and certified are allowed to use beanbag shotguns. Beanbag rounds may only be used in a manner consistent with training provided by this department.

3) **Officers who have been trained and certified to use a beanbag shotgun and have been issued one must deploy with it during their shift.**

4) **Officers shall only use the beanbag shotgun when objectively reasonable.**

5) **Officers shall issue a verbal warning to the subject and fellow officers prior to deploying the beanbag shotgun.**

Officers shall issue a verbal warning to the subject, other officers, and other individuals present, that a beanbag shotgun will be used and defer using the beanbag shotgun a reasonable amount of time to allow the subject to comply with the warning.

Exception: A verbal warning is required only if feasible and unless giving the warning would compromise the safety of the officer or others.

6) **Officers shall consider the risk of the beanbag shotgun round causing serious harm when determining whether to deploy.**

7) **Officers shall not target a subject's head, neck, or genital area.**

Officers shall not target the head or neck unless deadly force is justified.

In circumstances where deadly force is not justified, officers should direct the beanbag round toward the following areas:

- Lower abdomen, at belt level

- Buttocks

- Arms below the elbows

- Thigh

- Legs below the knee

8) **Authorized Use, Prohibitions, and Cautions.**

- Beanbag rounds may only be used on an individual engaged in active aggression or to prevent imminent physical harm to the officer or another person.

- Beanbag rounds should not be shot through glass or a chainlink fence due to the likelihood of rupturing the beanbags and having the contents injure others.

- All less lethal shotguns must be stored in the trunk or rear storage area of patrol vehicles.

- Officers are cautioned that the target area for a beanbag round substantially differs from a deadly force target area. Instead of aiming for the center mass of the body, beanbag shotguns are aimed at the lower abdomen, thighs, or forearms.

- Officers should be aware that targeting the chest has on occasion proven lethal when beanbag round is fired at a close range of less than twenty-one to thirty feet.

- Officers are further cautioned that the accuracy of the rounds decreases significantly after approximately forty-five feet. Their flight becomes erratic, striking objects to the right, left, or below the target, increasing the risk to innocent bystanders.

9)   Tactical Considerations.

- The optimal distance for a beanbag is between twenty-one and forty-five feet. The beanbag rounds present a risk of death or serious physical injury when fired at the chest, head, neck, and groin.

- Officers should also be prepared to employ other means to control the individual — including, if necessary, other force options consistent with department policy—if the individual does not respond sufficiently to the beanbag and cannot otherwise be subdued.

10)   Officers are prohibited from using beanbag rounds on an individual in a crowd without the approval of a supervisor.

Officers are prohibited from using beanbag rounds against an individual in a crowd unless the officer has the approval of a supervisor and can:

- Target a specific individual who poses an immediate threat of causing imminent physical harm, and

- Reasonably ensure that other individuals in the crowd who pose no threat of violence will not be struck by the weapon

11)   Officers must justify each separate beanbag shotgun use in their use-of-force statement.

12)   Officers are required to report each use of the beanbag shotgun (e.g., each time the beanbag shotgun is aimed at a subject and each round fired) regardless of whether a subject is struck.

13) All shotguns firing beanbag rounds must be painted in a bright color or otherwise marked clearly so as to make them instantly distinguishable from a shotgun firing live rounds.

14) Officers shall summon medical aid for all subjects who have been struck by a bean-bag round.

15) Beanbag shotgun inspections will be conducted on a semiannual basis to ensure that all are operable, and any necessary maintenance or repairs will be performed.

FIREARMS

1) Officers shall only shoot firearms in situations where deadly force is justified.

2) Officers shall only carry and use department-approved firearms, except in exigent circumstances.

3) Officers must pass an annual Firearms Qualification.

4) Officers shall not use firearms as impact weapons.

5) An officer may draw or exhibit a firearm in the line of duty when the officer has reasonable cause to believe it may be necessary for his or her own safety or for the safety of others.

   When an officer determines that the threat is over, the officer shall holster his or firearm.

   Unnecessarily or prematurely drawing or exhibiting a firearm may limit an officer's alternatives in controlling a situation, may create unnecessary anxiety on the part of citizens, and may result in an unwarranted or accidental discharge of the firearm.

   Officers shall not draw or exhibit a firearm unless the circumstances surrounding the incident create a reasonable belief that it may be necessary to use the firearm in conformance with this policy on the use of firearms.

6) Officers shall not fire warning shots.

7) Officers shall issue a verbal warning to the subject and fellow officers prior to shooting a firearm.

   Officers shall issue a verbal warning to the subject, other officers, and other individuals present, that a firearm will be shot and defer shooting the firearm for a reasonable amount of time to allow the subject to comply with the warning.

   Exception: A verbal warning is required only if feasible and unless giving the warning would compromise the safety of the officer or others.

8) **Officers shall not fire at or from a moving vehicle.**

Firing at a moving vehicle is generally prohibited, because doing so is often ineffective and may cause significant safety risks to the driver, passengers, and bystanders. Firearms shall not be discharged at a moving vehicle unless a person in the vehicle is immediately threatening the officer or another person with deadly force by means other than the vehicle. The moving vehicle itself shall not presumptively constitute a threat that justifies an officer's use of deadly force.

An officer threatened by an oncoming vehicle shall, if feasible, move out of its path instead of discharging a firearm at it or any of its occupants.

Officers shall not discharge a firearm from a moving vehicle unless a person is immediately threatening the officer or another person with deadly force.

Note: It is understood that the policy in regards to discharging a firearm at or from a moving vehicle may not cover every situation that may arise. In all situations, department members are expected to act with intelligence and exercise sound judgment, attending to the spirit of this policy. Any deviations from the provisions of this policy shall be examined rigorously on a case-by-case basis. The involved officers must be able to articulate clearly the reasons for the use of deadly force.

Factors that may be considered include:

- Whether the officer's life or the lives of others were in immediate peril, and

- Whether there was no reasonable or apparent mean of escape

9) **Pointing a firearm at a person is reportable force.**

Officers shall document all incidents where they point a firearm at a person.

Unholstering or displaying a firearm—including in a low-ready position—without pointing it at a person is not reportable force.

IMPACT WEAPONS

The baton is capable of delivering powerful blows to interrupt or incapacitate an aggressive subject. It is also capable of delivering lethal or permanently disabling blows.

1) **Education and Training Section (ETS) will train and certify Officers on department-approved impact weapons every two years.**

Officers will be trained and certified to use department-approved impact weapons before being authorized to carry these weapons.

2)   **Officers shall only use impact weapons when objectively reasonable.**

3)   **Officers will not use impact weapons on subjects who are restrained and under control, or are complying with police direction.**

4)   **A hard strike to the head with any impact weapon, including a baton, is prohibited unless deadly force is justified.**

     The head, throat, neck, spine, groin, or kidneys shall not be targeted unless deadly force is justified. Unintentional or mistaken blows to these areas must be reported to ensure that all reasonable care was taken to avoid them.

     Preferred target areas include arms, legs, and torso.

5)   **Officers shall not use flashlights as impact weapons, except in exigent circumstances.**

     The improvised use of weapons, such as flashlights, may present a greater risk of injury than batons. Use of another object in place of the baton, including flashlights, is prohibited unless there is an immediate need to strike and an officer is precluded from using or cannot feasibly use the conducted electrical weapon (CEW), baton, or oleoresin capsicum (OC) spray.

     The failure to carry a baton, in and of itself, does not justify the regular use of a flashlight as an impact weapon. Routine reliance on flashlights as an impact weapon is prohibited.

6)   **Officers must justify each separate impact weapon application in their use-of-force report.**

     Officers are required to report the use of an impact weapon to their sergeant, regardless of whether a subject is struck.

Exhibit 8

Photo of Officer Gray's Facial Bruises

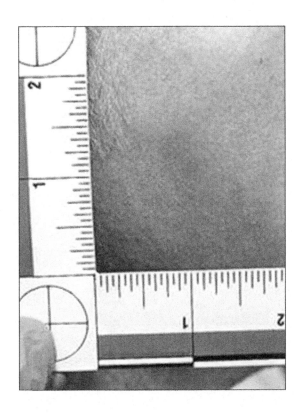

Exhibit 9

Officer Gray's Incident Report

Nita City Police Department					
Incident Report					
Date of Offense: August 9, YR-1	**Time:** 1150 Hrs	**Officer:** PII Darren Gray	**Arrest #:** N/A	**York #:** YR-1-084395	
Victim: PII Darren Gray	**D.O.B.:** 08/30/YR-28	**A.K.A. 1:** N/A	**Height:** 5'10"	**Weight:** 185 lbs	
Location of Arrest: 3000 blk Cranfield Drive	**City:** Nita City	**County:** Darrow	**State:** Nita	**Zip:** 11011	
Type of Incident: Disorderly Conduct	**Complainant:** On View	**Suspect(s):** Rudy York/ Johnny Pesky	**Court Date:** N/A	**York Disposition:** Open – CID Investigating	

Narrative:

I am writing this police report under orders. I reserve the right to modify this report at some time in the future. My attorney and I have discussed this, and I am not willing to waive my rights towards self-incrimination.

On August 9, YR-1, I was assigned to Beat 1A. This includes the area of Cranfield Drive in Nita City, Nita. I was on my way to sick baby call. When I was driving east in the 3000 block of Cranfield Drive, I had to slow down because two people later identified as Johnny Pesky and Rudy York were walking in the travel portion of the roadway. This road is separated by a double yellow line and there are sidewalks on both sides of the street.

Because I was on my way to a call, I decided to just ask the two people to move along onto the sidewalk. I was able to slowly move my marked patrol car to the right and come up next to the pair with my window rolled down. They seemed startled to see me and one of them used some profanity. At that time, I said something to the effect of "Hey guys, do me a favor and move to the sidewalk." Rudy York used more profanity, stating that he was just going up the street, and I asked him to go up the street using the sidewalk.

I started pulling away and I heard one or both of them yelling at me to mind my own business, while once again using profanity. I was not that far off, so I stopped my car and backed up, with the intention of telling them to just walk on the sidewalk. When I did, Rudy York closed the distance between himself and the car and held the door with his body while he was yelling something at me. I tried to open the door, but I could not and Rudy York reached into the car and grabbed me. I move to my right while inside the car and Rudy York came into the police car and just started hitting me. Because of the equipment in the car, I could not strike back. Rudy York was just in a rage and continued hitting me.

I reached up with my left hand and grabbed York below his neck, trying to push him away from me. This only made York more upset and he started hitting me on my face and head. He was pretty strong and some of the blows were making me blackout a little. I realized that York was then reaching down for my gun. I do not know if he grabbed my gun, but it seemed to me he did. At this point, I was in fear that I would lose consciousness and York would have my gun. I was in fear for my life, so I reached for my gun and started yelling that he back away or I would shoot. I was able to get my gun out of the holster and he was grabbing my hand, while still hitting me. I yelled several times I was going to shoot and then managed to fire a round.

York let go and started running away. I have no idea where Pesky was at this point, but I was able to get out of my car and yelled at the fleeing felon to stop. I was in fear that York was a threat to injure others, so I tried to prevent his escape and fired two or three rounds while yelling all the while that he stop. York did stop and turn around. I was yelling at him to get down on the ground, but he did not comply. At this point, he was about thirty feet away. I yelled several more times for him to get on the ground. York raised his arms and then yelled that he was going to take my gun away from me and started coming towards me. I yelled for him to stop but he kept coming and started coming faster. He then reached down with his right arm as if he was reaching for a gun. Fearing again for my life, I crouched down into a shooting position and started firing my service weapon. I continued firing at center mass until the threat was stopped. As soon as the threat was over, I stopped firing and contacted dispatch immediately. I then complied with all orders. I was also transported to Darrow County General Hospital, where I was treated for my injuries. Luckily, I do not have anything broken.

I will state with certainty that I only used the force that was necessary to stop the attack and I hate that I had to shoot my gun at all. I was in fear for my life, and this was the only reason why I fired my service weapon. This was the first and only time I ever fired my weapon while on duty. I did so in accordance with the training I received in the police academy and in in-service annual certifications. **NFI at this time.**

Officer Signature *Darren Gray*	**Date Signed:** Aug 10, YR-1	**Supervisor Review:** **MHJ**	**Date Reviewed:** Aug 10, YR-1

Shot in right eye
shot chest
right arm

Exhibit 10

CORONER OF DARROW COUNTY

GROSS AUTOPSY RECORD

Post-Mortem Examination

Name of Deceased: YORK, RUDY

Date/Time of Medical Examiner Notification: 8/9/YR-1 1:30:00 PM

Date/Time of Pathologist's Examination: 8/10/YR-1 8:00AM

Date/Time of Pronounced Death: 8/9/YR-1, 12:15:00 PM

Depth of Investigation (Pathologist): Complete Autopsy by Dr. L. Bader

Police Agency: Nita City Police Department (Complaint No.: YR-1-084395)

Scene: Dr. Louis Bader and Investigator Delgado were contacted by telephone at 1:30 p.m. on August 9, YR-1, and informed that a police shooting on had occurred at 2947 Cranfield Drive in Nita City. Our office was requested to come to the scene and retrieve the body and conduct a criminal autopsy examination. We immediately left and arrived at the scene of the shooting at 2:10 p.m., where we were met by Sergeant Goodman and Officer Gringsty. Sergeant Goodman directed both Investigator Delgado and me to the body, which was lying face down in the street under a white sheet. After Sergeant Goodman conducted a scene examination for evidence and after we examined the body and items of clothing, Sergeant Goodman released the body to our office and we returned with the body to office. The next morning at 8:00 a.m., I began my autopsy examination.

External Examination: The body is clothed in a pair of yellow socks with black leaves, brown shorts with pockets, blue underwear, a gray short sleeved t-shirt (with defects), and a black cloth belt. The appearance of age is approximately as stated. The body weight is 289 pounds, and the body length is 77 inches. The state of preservation is good in this unembalmed body. Rigor mortis is well developed. The body is heavier than ideal weight base upon height (BMI 34.2 kg/m2). Lividity is difficult to access due to natural skin pigmentation. There is no peripheral edema present. Personal hygiene is good. No unusual odor is detected as the body is examined. There is no abnormal skin pigmentation present. There is no external lymphadenopathy present. The hair is brown. The hair is worn short to medium length. There is a goatee present on the face. The body hair is of normal male distribution. The pupil of the left eye is round, regular, equal, and dilated. The scleral and conjunctival surfaces of the left eye are unremarkable. The right eye cannot be accessed due to an acute traumatic injury (gunshot wound). The iris of the left eye is brown. The teeth are in a fair state of repair. The gums are normal in appearance. The oral cavity is normal in appearance. There are no injuries of the tongue. The nose is symmetrical, and bloody fluid is present within the air passages. The external ears are normal in appearance and without injury. The neck is symmetrical and without masses or unusual mobility. The male breasts are normal in appearance. The abdomen is slightly protuberant, with the presence of stretch marks. Prior to the acute injury of the chest, the chest and back were symmetrical with normal conformation. Prior to the acute injuries of the right arm, the upper and lower extremities were symmetrical throughout. The hands are covered with brown paper bags. There is a scar present near the left chest that measures 0.2 cm in

National Institute for Trial Advocacy

43

greatest dimension. There is a scar present near the right upper abdomen that measures 0.5 cm in greatest dimension. There is a scar present near the elbow joint of the right arm that measures 1.0 cm in greatest dimension. There is a scar present near the right thigh that measures 0.3 cm in greatest dimension. There is a scar present near the right knee that measures 1.0 cm in greatest dimension. There are scattered scars present near the left knee that range in size from 0.5 to 1.0 cm in greatest dimension. There are two scars present near the lower left leg that range in size from 0.2 to 4.0 cm in greatest dimension. There are tattoos present on the body: right shoulder ("Kelle"), right forearm ("Big Rudy"), and left forearm ("Dre"). The acute gunshot injuries of the right arm, chest, and head are described below. The injuries of the external body surfaces are described below.

Injuries: There is a gunshot entrance wound of the vertex of the scalp. There is a gunshot entrance wound of the central forehead. There is a gunshot exit wound of the right jaw. There is a gunshot entrance wound of the upper right chest. There is a gunshot entrance wound of the lateral right chest. There is a gunshot entrance wound of the upper ventral right arm. There is a gunshot exit wound of the upper dorsal right arm. There is a gunshot entrance wound of the dorsal right forearm. There is a gunshot exit wound of the medial ventral right forearm. There is a tangential (graze) gunshot wound of the right bicep. There is a tangential (graze) gunshot wound near the ventral surface of the right thumb. There is a gunshot-related defect present near the right eyebrow that measures 4.0 x 2.0 cm. There is a gunshot-related defect present near the right eyelid that measures 3.0 x 1.0 cm. There is an abrasion present near the right forehead that measures 7.0 cm in greatest dimension. There is a dried abrasion present near the lateral right face that measures 3.5 cm in greatest dimension. There is an abrasion present near the upper right cheek that measures 3.0 cm in greatest dimension. There are scattered abrasions present near the lateral right surface of the lower lip that range in size from 0.1 to 0.2 cm in greatest dimension. There is an abrasion present near the upper right chest that measures 2.5 cm in greatest dimension. There is an area of abrasions present near the right hip that measures 1.0 x 0.2 cm. There is a dried abrasion present near the left thumb that measures 0.2 cm in greatest dimension. There is an abrasion present near the dorsal surface of the left wrist that measures 2.0 x 1.5 cm. There is a focal area of discoloration present near the dorsal surface of the 5th left finger that measures 0.2 cm in greatest dimension. There is a linear abrasion present near the ventral surface of the left forearm that measures 3.5 cm in greatest dimension. There are scattered postmortem abrasions present on the hands.

Detailed Description of Specified Injuries

#1. There is a gunshot entrance wound of the vertex of the scalp. This wound is located 20.0 cm above the level of the right external auditory meatus and near midline of the vertex of the head. The hole measures 10 mm x 8 mm. It is round with level edges. The edges focally show an abrasion ring measuring up to 1 mm in greatest dimension, which is most prominent near the superior edge of the wound. No powder stipple is identified. No soot is identified. The wound track shows deeper hemorrhage. A bullet, seen on x-rays, is found within the soft tissue of the right face and is recovered and submitted as evidence. There is internal beveling of the defect in the parietal bone of the skull. Evaluation of this wound indicates that it is an entrance wound. The path of this shot is downward and rightward. The track of this bullet has been traced to pass via the scalp, soft tissue, parietal bone of the skull, right parietal lobe of the brain, right temporal lobe of the brain, and right temporal bone of the skull, to rest within the soft tissue of the lateral right face. Passage of the bullet through the head created fractures of the calvarial and basilar bones of the skull. Pneumocephalus is present (confirmed on postmortem x-ray examination). Subdural and subarachnoid hemorrhage is present on the convexities of the brain. There are small, punctate contusions present within the white matter of the brain near the path of the gunshot injury. The gunshot injury path, through the brain, is approximately 12 cm in length.

#2. There is a gunshot entrance wound of the central forehead. This wound is located 7.0 cm above the level of the right external auditory meatus and 2.0 cm right of the anterior midline of the head. The hole measures 15 mm x 10 mm. It is oval with slightly inverted edges. The edges show an abrasion ring measuring up to 3 mm in greatest dimension, which is most prominent near the superior edge of the wound. No powder stipple is identified. No soot is identified. The wound track shows deeper hemorrhage. X-rays show small bullet fragments associated with this wound; however, due to their small size, they are not recovered as evidence. This wound pairs with the wound of the right jaw described immediately below, which is an exit wound. The path of the shot is downward, slightly backward, and rightward. The track of this bullet has been traced to pass via the skin, soft tissue, right eye, inferior right orbital bone, and soft tissue of the face, to exit the skin of the right jaw. Passage of the bullet through the head/face created fractures of the facial bones. There are irregular, gunshot-related defects associated with the passage of the bullet through the head/face that are present near the right eyelid and right eyebrow. The dimensions of these gunshot-related defects have already been described above.

#3. There is a gunshot exit wound of the right jaw. This wound is located 5.5 cm below the level of the right external auditory meatus, 11.0 cm right of the anterior midline of the head. The hole measures 15 mm x 9 mm. It is irregular with clean edges. Evaluation of this wound indicates that it is an exit wound. This wound pairs with the wound of the central forehead described immediately above, which is an entrance wound.

#4. There is a gunshot entrance wound of the upper right chest. This wound is located 16.0 cm below the level of the right external auditory meatus and 9.0 cm right of the anterior midline of the chest. The hole measures 15 mm x 10 mm. It is oval with level edges. Edges show an abrasion ring measuring up to 2 mm in greatest dimension and are most prominent near the superior/inferior borders of the wound. No powder stipple is identified. No soot is identified. The wound track shows deeper hemorrhage. A bullet, seen on x rays, is found within the soft tissue of the right chest and is recovered and submitted as evidence. Evaluation of this wound indicates that it is an entrance wound. The path of this shot is slightly downward and backward. The track of this bullet has been traced to pass via the skin, soft tissue, right clavicle, upper lobe of the right lung, to rest near the soft tissue of the posterior third right intercostal space. The passage of the bullet through the upper lobe of the right lung created a 2 cm defect.

#5. There is a gunshot entrance wound of the lateral right chest. This wound is located 20.0 cm below the level of the right external auditory meatus and 22.0 cm right of the anterior midline of the chest. The hole measures 12 mm x 12 mm. It is round. The edges show an abrasion ring measuring up to 1 mm in greatest dimension, which is most prominent near the lateral edges of the wound. No powder stipple is identified. No soot is identified. The wound track shows deeper hemorrhage. A bullet, seen on x-rays, is found within the soft tissue of the lateral right back and is recovered and submitted as evidence. Evaluation of this wound indicates that it is an entrance wound. The path of this shot is downward and backward. The track of this bullet has been traced to have passed via the skin, soft tissue, and eighth right rib to rest within the soft tissue of the lateral right back. The passage of the bullet near/through the eighth right rib created a fracture of the same and subsequently created a bony defect that punctured the lower lobe of the right lung. The puncture wound within the lower lobe of the right lung measures 0.5 cm in greatest dimension.

#6. There is gunshot entrance wound of the upper ventral right arm. This wound is located 20.0 cm below the level of the right shoulder and 1.0 cm right of the anterior midline of the upper right arm. The hole measures 10 mm x 10 mm. It is oval. The edges do not definitively show an abrasion ring. There is a focal area of contusion found around the wound edge that measures up to 1 mm in greatest dimension. No powder stipple is identified. No soot is identified. The wound track shows deeper hemorrhage. X-rays show no lead or bullet fragments associated with this wound. This wound pairs with the wound of the upper dorsal right arm described immediately below, which is an exit wound. Evaluation of this wound indicates that it is an entrance wound. The path of this shot is slightly upward, backward, and leftward. The track of this bullet has been traced to pass via the skin, soft tissue to exit the skin of the upper dorsal right arm.

#7. There is gunshot exit wound of the upper dorsal right arm. This wound is located 19.0 cm below the level of the right shoulder and 7.0 cm left of the posterior midline of the right upper arm. The hole measures 18 mm x 10 mm. It is elongated with clean edges. Evaluation of this wound indicates that it is an exit wound. This wound pairs with the wound of the upper ventral right arm described immediately above, which is an entrance wound.

#8. There is a gunshot entrance wound of the dorsal right forearm. This wound is located 16.0 cm below the level of the right elbow and 2.0 cm right of the posterior midline of the right forearm. The hole measures 11 mm x 10 mm. It is oval with slightly inverted edges. The edges show an abrasion ring measuring up to 1 mm in greatest dimension, which is most prominent near the lateral edge of the wound. No soot is identified. No powder stipple is identified. The wound track shows deeper hemorrhage. X-rays show small bullet fragments associated with this wound; however, due to their small size, they are not recovered and submitted as evidence. Evaluation of this wound indicates that it is an entrance wound. This wound pairs with the wound of the medial ventral right forearm described immediately below, which is an exit wound. The path of this shot is slightly upward, forward, and leftward. The track of this bullet has been traced to have passed via the skin, soft tissue, right ulna, and soft tissue, to exit the ventral medial right forearm. Passage of the bullet through the right ulna created a fracture of the same.

#9. There is a gunshot exit wound of the medial ventral right forearm. This wound is located 15.0 cm below the level of the right elbow and 5.0 cm to the left of the anterior midline of the right forearm. The hole measures 20 mm x 20 mm. It is irregular with clean edges. There is slight extrusion of soft tissue from the wound edge. Evaluation of this wound indicates that it is an exit wound. This wound pairs with the wound of the dorsal right forearm described immediately above, which is an entrance wound.

#10. There is a tangential (graze) gunshot wound of the right bicep. This wound is located 6.0 cm above the level of the right elbow and 2. 0 cm left of the anterior midline of the upper right arm. The wound measures 3.0 x 1.0 cm. It is oriented, approximately, in a 9 o'clock to 3 o'clock position. It is flat/shallow in depth and elongated in shape. The edges are dried and discolored. No powder stipple is identified. The exact directional path of the bullet cannot be easily determined.

#11. There is a tangential (graze) gunshot wound near the ventral surface of the right thumb. This wound is located 5.0 cm below the level of the right wrist and 4.0 cm right of the ventral midline of the right hand. The wound measures 5.0 x 2.0 cm. It is oriented, approximately, in a 12 o'clock to 6 o'clock position. It is elongated with dried edges and associated with skin tags. The skin tags point towards the tip of the right thumb. The path of the track is upwards. No powder stipple is identified. There is a focal area of discoloration near the ventral surface of the base of the right thumb.

Body Cavities: The body is opened with the usual Y-shaped thoracoabdominal and bitemporal scalpel incisions. The anterior thoracic musculature and subcutaneous regions show hemorrhage to match the previously described gunshot wounds. The peritoneal cavity shows no abnormalities. The left pleural cavity is unremarkable. The right pleural cavity contains 400 ml of blood. The retroperitoneum is unremarkable. The pericardial cavity is not remarkable.

Neck Organs: The soft tissue of the neck is free of hemorrhage. The hyoid bone is intact and is cartilaginous. The glottis and laryngeal and tracheal airways are patent and contain patchy areas of hemorrhage. The larynx is normal and is well cartilaginous. The thyroid gland is pale in appearance. The parathyroids are not identified.

Mediastinum: There is a residual amount of fatty thymic tissue present that is white tan and weighs 10 gm. The mediastinum is normal in appearance.

Heart: The heart weighs 400 gm. The left ventricular wall thickness measures 1.4 cm, and the right ventricular wall thickness measures 0.3 cm. The surface of the heart is smooth, glistening, and transparent. The wall is of normal consistency. There is a normal amount of subepicardial fat tissue present. The size and contours of the heart are normal. The endocardium, cardiac valves, and chambers are not remarkable. The coronary arteries are thin walled and of normal diameter throughout. The cut surface of the myocardium is a pale reddish brown color.

Vascular System: The aorta and arterial system are not remarkable. The systemic veins are normal in appearance.

Lungs: The acute injury of the right lung has already been described above. The lungs together weigh 600 gm. The lung surface is gray-brown and red. The lung tissue throughout is spongy and crepitant. The air passages are lined by smooth, pink mucosa and focally contain patchy areas of blood. The cut surfaces of the lungs show areas of intraparyenchymal hemorrhage present near the previously described areas of gunshot injury and rib fracture. The remaining areas of pulmonary parenchyma are unremarkable. The pulmonary artery and veins are free of emboli and thrombi.

Liver: The liver weighs 1250 gm. It is pale red-brown and of normal consistency. The cut surface of the liver is normal except for the pale color of the liver parenchyma.

Biliary Tract: The gallbladder and biliary tract are normal and free of stones.

Pancreas: The pancreas is normal in consistency and in appearance.

Gastrointestinal Tract: The entire gastrointestinal tract is examined and found normal. The stomach contains scant gastric contents. There are focal areas of hyperemia present on the mucosal surface of the stomach.

Spleen: The spleen weighs 150 gm and is normal on the surface and cut section.

Lymphatic System: The lymph nodes are normal in size and appearance.

Bone Marrow: The bone marrow is normal.

Adrenals: The adrenals are well supplied with lipoid material and are free of hemorrhage, inflammation, and primary and secondary neoplasm. The medullary portions are not remarkable.

Kidneys: The kidneys appear grossly of normal configuration and together weigh 300 gm. The cortex measures 0.7 cm in thickness. The renal capsules strip with ease to reveal a normally smooth surface. The surface is a pale reddish-brown color. There is a small simple cyst within the medullary region of the left kidney that measures 1.0 cm in greatest dimension. The cyst contains brownish-colored fluid. The remaining areas of the kidney parenchyma show no abnormalities. The papilla and ureters are not remarkable.

Bladder: The bladder contains 40 ml of yellow urine. The wall is entirely normal.

Male Genital System: There is foreskin present near the head of the penis. The remaining male genitalia system is unremarkable.

Cranial Cavity: The acute gunshot injuries of the head have already been described above. The reflected scalp shows hemorrhage to match the previously described gunshot wounds. The gunshot related fractures of the calvarium and bones at the base of the skull have already been described above. The dura mater is normal in appearance except for the previously described gunshot. The weight of the unfixed brain is 1350 gm. The areas of subarachnoid hemorrhage and subdural hemorrhage present within the intracranial cavity have already been described above. Cut sections reveal that prior to the acute injury there were essentially normal structures throughout. The focal, punctate contusions present within the white matter have already been described above. The cerebrovasculature is free of atherosclerosis. The pituitary gland is grossly normal. The pineal gland is not identified.

Spinal Cord: The upper spinal cord as viewed from the cranial cavity is not remarkable.

Special Studies/Specimens Obtained: Urine, vitreous humor, chest blood, liver, and brain are sent for toxicology. The previously described recovered bullets, blood stain card, fingernail clippings, fingernail scrapings, fingernail clippers, swabs of the hands, clothing, and a leafy green substance are submitted to the Darrow County Sheriff's Laboratory as evidence.

Comment: The histology examination will be issued as a supplemental report.

Tissue fragment: Sections of the tissue fragment from the exterior surface of the police officer's motor vehicle are consistent with a fragment of skin overlying soft (connective) tissue. There are features of desiccation/drying artifact present within the soft tissue. There is a granular present. Focally lightly pigmented keratinocytes are present within the basal layer of the stratified squamous epithelium.

Medical Examiner: *Louis Bader*

Date: *8/19/YR-1*

Gunshot Wounds

Medical Examiner: _Louis Bader_

Date: _8/19/YR-1_

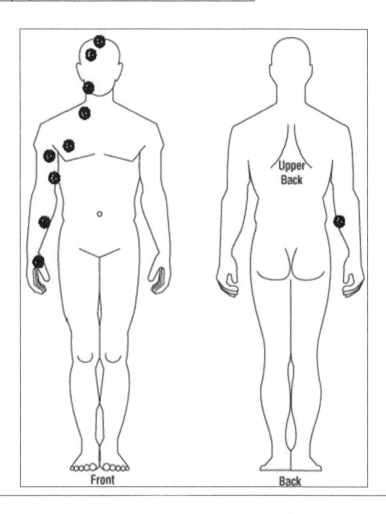

Exhibit 11

Denny Galehouse's Map of Scene

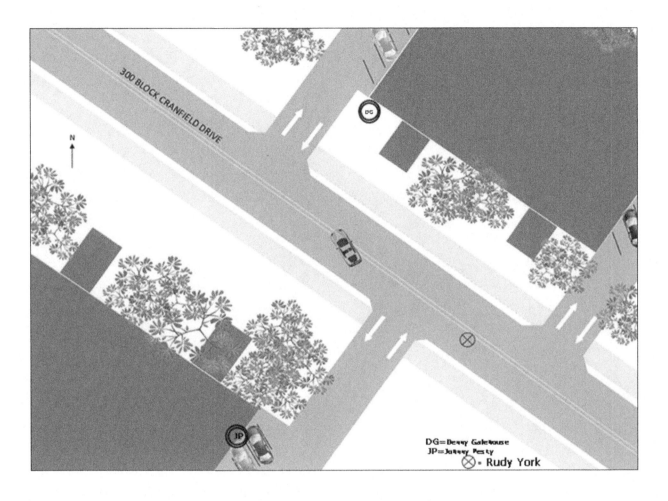

Exhibit 12

Dr. Mel Parnell's Diagram

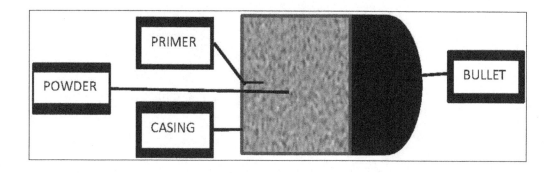

LAW ENFORCEMENT REPORTS

NITA CITY POLICE DEPARTMENT
OFFENSE REPORT

FILE NUMBER:	YR-1-084395
VICTIM:	Rudy York
SUSPECT:	Officer Darren Gray
LOCATION:	2947 Cranfield Drive
	Nita City, Nita
OFFENSE:	CC 187—Murder
DATE OF REPORT:	August 10, YR-1
BY:	Detective Sergeant Billy Goodman
	Badge Number 114

Details of Offense

My Notification and Arrival at the Scene

At 1302 hours, I was at the Nita City Police Department and received a call from dispatch that there was a homicide where an officer discharged his weapon and shot a male who had been pronounced dead at the scene near 2947 Cranfield Drive. I then drove to the scene and arrived at 1330 hours, whereupon I saw a crowd of bystanders and two uniformed officers, Officer Darren Gray and Officer Renata Gringsty.

Officer Gray immediately said that he was attacked, beaten, and that the dead man later identified as Rudy York lying in the street at one point had tried to get Officer Gray's weapon and was advancing toward him to kill him when Officer Gray shot him multiple times. He said that York and another man were walking down the middle of Cranfield Drive and Officer Gray told them to get off the street and walk on the sidewalk. He said as he was trying to get out of his vehicle, York did not allow him to open his car door and a struggle began with York, who tried to get his weapon, and Officer Gray fired one shot. He said that York ran away with the other man and Officer Gray gave chase on foot. He said York then turned around and began to run toward Officer Gray, who then began firing his weapon to stop York from further assaulting him. He said that York did not display a weapon, and Officer Gray did not know where the second male went.

Officer Gringsty said she had arrived a few minutes before I had and she was trying to control the bystanders and was taping the scene to protect any important evidence from being destroyed. She said that she had not observed any shootings, and when she arrived the dead man was already lying in the street. She immediately looked at the dead man, and when she was sure that he was lifeless, she retrieved a white blanket and placed it over his body so that no one would tamper with any evidence. She did not observe any members of the crowd touching any of the objects in the street or touching the dead man lying in the street.

I contacted the Darrow County Crime Lab and advised that office that we had an officer shooting homicide and we needed their expert services. The dispatch operator informed me that they had already been advised and Whitney Moses was on the way to the scene. Moses arrived just a few minutes later. I assisted Officer Gringsty and Moses in preserving the scene.

I then directed Officer Gray to return immediately to our headquarters and told him that what appeared to be minor injuries to his head should be treated. I also told him to complete a police report detailing the incident and report to Assistant Chief McFadden. Officer Gray waited until Officer Ellingsworth arrived in a squad car, and the two of them then returned to headquarters. Some of the bystanders were angry and shouting and at times yelled obscenities and threats.

The Scene and Evidence Found

The scene took place in the 2900 block of Cranfield Drive. This is within the Cranfield Green apartment complex. At the eastern end of the complex, the roadway changes names to Windward Court. Adjacent to the Canfield Green apartment complex, on the eastern side, is the Northwinds apartment complex. At the western end of Cranfield Drive, the 3000 block changes to single-family homes. Further west of the homes is the intersection of West Florissant Avenue and Cranfield Drive.

Whitney Moses and I directed our attention to the white Chevrolet Tahoe labeled "Police" on both sides in front of 2964 Cranfield Drive. It was parked at an angle in the westbound lane facing north, with its left front tire nearly on the double yellow line. All four doors were closed, and three of the windows were closed. The driver's window was open, with pieces of broken glass on the ground and inside the vehicle. The driver's side mirror was bent toward the front of the vehicle. There appeared to be human tissue on the upper exterior driver's door, and that door had a bulge protruding out with a small amount of paint missing. There appeared to be a small amount of blood on the exterior rear driver's side door in the middle of the door just above the "Police" decal.

We then directed our attention to the road around the police vehicle and saw the following items:

- A yellow/black/white bracelet was near the front driver's side tire

- A baseball cap, upside down, was south of the front driver's side tire

- Broken glass just south of the front driver's side door

- A single spent cartridge casing head stamped "FEDERAL 40 S&W" was just south of the rear driver's side door

- A single spent cartridge casing head stamped "FEDERAL 40 S&W" was along the southern curb, south of the police vehicle

- A brown bracelet was under the vehicle behind the front passenger side tire

We then walked southeast on Cranfield Drive from the white Chevrolet Tahoe in the southwest lane of traffic and found a black and white Nike sandal positioned upside down, with the toe facing northwest. Further southeast in the southeast-bound lane near the double yellow line was the matching sandal positioned right side up facing south.

We next went to the area where the body of Rudy York lay on Cranfield Drive in front of 2943 Cranfield Drive. His body was covered with a white cover located in the center of the roadway. Northwest of the police Tahoe in the northwest lane were what appeared to be blood droplets running from just west from Coppercreek Court to the body.

West of that location were two spent "FEDERAL 40 S&W" cartridges in the middle of the road.

East from there in the southeast lane on Cranfield Drive close to the curb were two more spent cartridge casings stamped "FEDERAL 40 S&W."

Just east of there was another spent cartridge casing stamped "FEDERAL 40 S&W."

South of that cartridge in the grass area between the southeast lane of Cranfield Drive and the sidewalk were four spent casings stamped "FEDERAL 40 S&W."

Northeast of the body in the northwest lane of Cranfield Drive was an apparent projectile.

South of the body in the southeast lane on Cranfield Drive just east of Caddiefield Road was a spent cartridge casing stamped "FEDERAL 40 S&W."

Full details of the locations of the items described in this report can be seen on the diagram, which our office prepared and labeled as Rudy York Shooting Scene.

The Body

Around 1400 hours, I contacted the Coroner's Office and spoke to both Coroner's Investigator Delgado and Forensic Pathologist Dr. Louis Bader. I requested that they come to the scene, and they arrived around 1430 hours. I met with them briefly and then directed their attention to Rudy York's body. They conducted their investigation in my presence. Investigator Delgado removed the white cover, and they removed identification. York was face-down, he was wearing a light gray t-shirt, blue underwear, khaki shorts, a black belt, tall yellow socks with apparent marijuana leaves on them. What appeared to be blood was on the roadway near York's head, his left arm was bent, and his left and right hands were empty. I observed no weapons on his body or near it. His body was moved to his back on the ground, and there were visible gunshot wounds to his right hand, right arm, head, and left forearm. Investigator Delgado removed two five-dollar bills from the deceased's right front pocket and a notepad. He also retrieved a red lighter and a black lighter from his left front pocket. At the conclusion, the body was placed in a secure body transportation bag and transported to the Darrow County Coroner's Office.

The Handling of Evidence

Throughout my investigation, I took photos of the scene; Officer's Chevrolet Tahoe at its position of rest, the body on the street, and Officer Gray's weapon, which he told me he used to shoot Rudy York. I directed Officer Gray to leave his weapon with me, and he turned it over to me. I later turned it over to Whitney Moses. No one else in my presence handled Officer Gray's weapon after that. Throughout my scene investigation, I made sure that the only people at the scene who touched evidentiary items were the forensic experts from the Darrow County Crime Lab and from the Coroner's Office. All of the items that were examined by Whitney Moses were booked and examined solely by Whitney Moses.

Some evidence that we pursued was unavailable:

- I directed my attention to an apartment building at 2960 Cranfield Drive and noticed on the north side of the building what appeared to be damage from a projectile to the vinyl siding above a window on the east side. Later, I attempted to extract a projectile, but I was unable to do so because the building was under construction, and extracting the projectile would have damaged the building.

- I checked with the apartment complex managers and area security companies, and learned that no security cameras were present or operated within the apartment complex.

Statement of Officer Gray

At 1535 hours, I had concluded my scene investigation and returned to headquarters. I met with Lieutenant Mantle, who directed me to take a statement from Officer Gray. I met with Officer Gray, who was accompanied by his attorney, Landon Mack, who had apparently been retained by the Nita City Police Officers Association. I could see several apparent injuries, particularly that the left and right sides of his face and his left ear were red and swollen. There were scratches were on the left side of his neck, and there was a large abrasion at the base of his neck. Because of my concern that Officer Gray required medical attention, I arranged for him to be transported to the Darrow County Medical Center. I drove both Officer Gray and his counsel to the hospital. I waited until he received treatment for his injuries. Then, in the presence of his counsel, Landon Mack, I asked Officer Gray if he would provide his account of the incident. He agreed to do so, and agreed to his statement being audio recorded. His statement was fully recorded digitally with a NCPD recorder. During the conversation, I made detailed notes, which I retained. The plan was to transfer the recording to a DVD. Unfortunately, following the recording of Officer Gray's statement, when we played the recorder back at the station, we learned that the batteries in the recorder were defective and we were totally unable to extract any portion of the recording to transfer to a DVD. The following account was the result of my extensive notes, and I believe it to be an accurate and complete account of Officer Gray's statement.

He said that he had been an officer with the department for five years and not once had he ever had to use his weapon. On August 8, YR-1, he had just completed an assignment, and after that assignment he was driving west on Cranfield Drive when he observed two unknown subjects walking toward his location from the area of Cranfield Drive and West Florissant Avenue. He described one as thin, about five and one-half feet tall, short hair wearing a black t-shirt, later identified as Johnny Pesky. The second he described as of medium build—about six feet and three inches and about 270 pounds—wearing a baseball cap, gray shirt, khaki shorts, and yellow socks, later identified as Rudy York.

He stopped his police vehicle, put his window down, waited until they walked by, and then he said, "Hey, guys, why don't you walk on the sidewalk?" The smaller one said, "We are almost to our destination." Then the big guy said, "The fuck with what you say." Both walked by his vehicle. Then he called dispatch and said he was conducting a pedestrian check. At that point, Officer Gray backed his vehicle and said, "Hey, come here."

When he opened his door, York slammed it shut. The officer then told York to get back and he tried to open the door again. York again slammed the door shut and placed both on his hands on the door, holding it shut. Officer Gray told York several times to get back and move away from the vehicle. York then thrust his body into the window and began punching Officer Gray multiple times in the chin, face, chest, and shoulders. Again, Officer Gray ordered him to stop. York then punched him with a closed fist on the on the right side of his face, which stunned him. Officer Gray reached for his mace in his duty belt, but he couldn't reach it. Also, he did not believe that his collapsible baton would be effective. At that point, he was overpowered and he could not escape through the passenger side, as the radio and computer would block him from getting out.

He was able to push York away far enough so he could reach his firearm with his right hand. Withdrawing it from his holster, he yelled, "Stop or I will shoot." York then grabbed the top of the gun and said, "You're too much of a pussy to shoot me." Officer Gray again ordered York to "get back," but York did not and Officer

Gray felt York's fingers moving toward the trigger, so he pulled the trigger but the weapon malfunctioned, probably because York's hand prevented the gun from firing. Officer Gray again pulled the trigger, and again it malfunctioned. He pulled the trigger a third time, and it discharged one round, which traveled through the driver's window. He saw the glass window shatter, and immediately he saw blood but he could not tell who was injured. At that point, York put his hand through the window and struck him several times with his fist, and then York fled east on Cranfield.

At this point, Officer Gray notified dispatch that shots were fired and requested assistance. He left his vehicle and chased York on foot, shouting verbal commands to stop, which York ignored. At this point, York stopped, turned around, and had an "intense and psychotic look on his face." He immediately placed his right hand into his waistband of his pants. At this point, Officer Gray stopped about 30 feet from York, had his hand on his firearm, and ordered York to get on the ground. York screamed something inaudible and then "charged" toward him. Officer Gray back-pedaled to keep the distance between them, as Officer Gray believed that if York reached him, he would again overpower him as he had done in his patrol vehicle.

York continued to ignore Officer Gray's commands and got within fifteen feet from him. Officer Gray then discharged five rounds to stop York. This did not slow York, who continued to advance, and Officer Gray discharge two additional rounds, and York continued to advance. York leaned forward as if to tackle Officer Gray, who then fired a final shot. York fell to the ground and did not get up again. Officer Gray called dispatch immediately and requested immediate assistance. While he waited for assistance, he inspected his firearm, ejected the empty magazine, and found one live cartridge in the chamber. Officer Gringsty arrived shortly after, and then I arrived. He said that when I arrived he remembers turning over the firearm and magazine to me. He said that after I directed him to return to headquarters, he waited for Officer Ellingsworth, who drove him back to the station, where he reported to Assistant Chief McFadden.

He explained that his injuries were painful, and that he would certainly inform our department of the nature of all of the injuries he suffered and make the medical reports from the hospital available after he receives copies from the hospital. That concluded Officer Gray's statement.

NITA CITY POLICE DEPARTMENT
SUPPLEMENTAL REPORT

FILE NUMBER:	YR-1-084395
VICTIM:	Rudy York
SUSPECT:	Officer Darren Gray
LOCATION:	2947 Cranfield Drive
	Nita City, Nita
OFFENSE:	CC 187—Murder
DATE OF REPORT:	August 12, YR-1
BY:	Detective Sergeant Billy Goodman
	Badge Number 114

On August 12, YR-1, at 1014 hours, I was contacted by Assistant Chief McFadden and informed that Johnny Pesky called dispatch to inquire whether he was going to be arrested in the case where Rudy York was killed. He wanted to explain that he had done nothing wrong. Chief McFadden told dispatch to inform Pesky that he should come to headquarters and contact me, as I was the chief investigator, and dispatch instructed Pesky to see me at 1100 hours.

At 1050, Johnny Pesky arrived at my office. I told him that we had no warrant out for him but we would like to get his side of the event. He said that he would fully cooperate with the police and would be glad to get the whole matter cleared up. He told me that he did not want the statement recorded, as some of "Big Rudy's friends" might not like him talking to the cops. I agreed, but I said I would have to take notes. He said that was "cool." He said that the community protests about a cop killing Big Rudy has made it difficult for him to be seen talking to the police, and that is why he kept a low profile.

When he started talking, he asked if we would arrest him after he described what happened. I repeated that we did not have a warrant out for him. I asked him if he had a criminal record, and he said that a couple of years ago he was falsely convicted for theft, which was a misdemeanor and he was and still is on probation. He asked again if he would be jailed for violating probation. I told him that was not our intention to prosecute him, but we needed his recollection of the shooting. I told him that after the interview he would be free to leave the station.

Johnny Pesky's Statement

He stated that he had known Rudy York as Big Rudy for several months, but they were not close friends. He said that because he was twenty-two years old and Big Rudy was only eighteen years old, he was someone who could possibly help Big Rudy get an education and make something of his life. He described how they'd had several discussions about jobs and education, but nothing had developed so far to help Big Rudy.

He had no idea whether Big Rudy had a criminal record, and he had no reason to believe that Big Rudy would break the law or be violent. He said the morning of the shooting Big Rudy had "smoked stuff," but he saw no symptoms of any irrational or violent behavior from Big Rudy. He admitted to me that he also uses marijuana and had on the morning of the shooting, but it had not affected him, either. Big Rudy wanted to get some cigarillos, and the two decided to go to the market on Florissant Street. On the way, they stopped and Big Rudy talked to some construction workers. After that, they walked toward the store. When they got there, it was closed. A sign on the door said the store would open later, which upset Big Rudy a bit, so they walked back toward their apartments.

When they were almost all the way home, a police car pulled up to them, Pesky said, and the cop said something about how they had to get over to the sidewalk. Big Rudy said something back to him. Pesky doesn't recall his words, but it was something like disagreeing with the officer. Pesky told the officer that they were almost home and thought that would be enough for them to get home OK. The officer left, and they continued walking in the street and suddenly he heard tires screeching, and he looked around and the officer had backed up to them, and he heard him say something, and that's when Big Rudy got upset.

Big Rudy walked over to the officer's car and said something that Pesky could not hear. Then Big Rudy charged the cop as the cop was trying to get out of his car. Big Rudy tried to grab the gun from him while the cop was trapped in his car. That was when Rudy got shot the first time by the cop. After that shot, Big Rudy ran away from the cop car. He then turned around and ran back toward the cop car. At this point, the cop was out of the care with his gun drawn and was yelling at Big Rudy to stop, telling told him to "get down on the ground or he would shoot." Big Rudy still ran right at the cop and yelled something like he was going to "take it from him." Pesky thinks that is the time the cop shot him several times. Rudy fell to the ground and did not get up.

I asked Pesky to describe how Big Rudy's hands were positioned when he was running toward the officer. He said that he remembers that Big Rudy had one or both hands up, but he put them down before he ran towards the officer. I then asked Pesky whether he saw Big Rudy shot in the back. He said that he believed at one point when Big Rudy was running away that one of the officer's shots may have hit him, but he couldn't be sure. I then asked him if he would describe the distance between the officer and Big Rudy when he was running toward the officer before Big Rudy fell. Pesky pointed to the wall and said it was about the distance from the wall to where Pesky was standing in my office. I later measured that distance—fourteen and one-half feet.

At the conclusion of Pesky's statement, I informed him that he would be a necessary witness if the case went to court. He said that he would prefer not to have to testify, as he has many friends who are upset that Big Rudy was killed by a cop. I told him that the police and the District Attorney's Office have not decided what, if any, charges should be filed, and one possibility may be that Officer Gray might be charged with a criminal offense. He said, "If that happens, I'll testify." He said he intended to get a lawyer. I told him that was his right, but I asked him that if he did retain a lawyer our office would appreciate that he let us know. That concluded our discussion.

On August 18, YR-1, at 1530 hours, I attended a meeting conducted by Assistant Chief McFadden and attended by police management. The issue of whether Officer Gray would be prosecuted was the main topic, along with discussions about the continued protests by community activists and the required conduct of officers controlling those protests. We were informed that a thorough analysis of the evidence by our office pointed to wrongful conduct by Officer Gray and the case was under review by the Darrow County District Attorney's Office, and that a decision whether criminal charges would be filed against Officer Gray would most probably be decided within the next two to three weeks.

At this meeting, there was a discussion about the protest problems that required overtime police officer duty for both daytime and night. These were the following protest groups:

- Lives Matter Action Committee

- The Anti-Police Citizens of Nita City

- Nita City Citizens urging that Mayor Andrews, District Attorney Haugstad, and Police Chief Brownston be fired

It was ascertained that a large majority of the protest organization members came from both the area where Rudy York resided and students primarily attending Nita State College and the University of Nita. Photos were taken of the pickets and protesters conducted in the streets in front of the Darrow County Courthouse on August 17, YR-1.

Just before the meeting concluded, it was announced that Captain Birdie Tebbetts, who is our department's commander of the Education and Training Division, had thoroughly reviewed the case and concluded that Officer Gray did not comply with numerous requirements under our department's Policy on the Use of Force and the Use of Force Continuum. The department and the District Attorney's Office are awaiting the results of the forensic examination conducted by Darrow County Crime Lab.

Our department's efforts to conduct a scene canvas to locate anyone who witnessed the shooting did not produce any eyewitnesses. The only witnesses were those who heard shots fired and then looked out from windows of the nearby apartments or homes. Many were greatly upset about the shooting and the police leaving the body in the street. Despite the notice our department sent to news media urging citizens living in the area or driving through who saw the shooting to please to contact the department, to date the only eyewitnesses to the shooting we have discovered are Officer Gray and Johnny Pesky.

NITA CITY POLICE DEPARTMENT
REPORT

FILE NUMBER:	YR-1-084395
VICTIM:	Rudy York
SUSPECT:	Officer Darren Gray
LOCATION:	2947 Cranfield Drive
	Nita City, Nita
OFFENSE:	CC 187—Murder
DATE OF REPORT:	August 17, YR-1
BY:	Captain Birdie Tebbetts, Division Commander of Shot Team
	Badge Number 92

On August 9, YR-1, at approximately 12:03 p.m., the Nita City Police Department dispatch supervisor sent a text to my Shot Team alerting us to the police-involved shooting. My team was on call on August 9. I was the Shot Team leader. My team consisted of Sergeant Wells from the State Police and Sergeant Cooper from the Darrow County Sheriff's Department.

I recommend that Officer Gray face charges because he used force that was greater than necessary for the incident and because he did not follow the use-of-force continuum policy. I would like to explain the reasoning behind my recommendation.

The Initial Contact with Rudy York

From the very beginning of this incident, Officer Gray failed to conduct himself in a proper way. He started the encounter in an adversarial fashion. This escalated the situation right from the beginning. Police officers are taught that they are part of the community. For officers to receive respect from others, they need to respect others first. Johnny Pesky's statement made it clear that Officer Gray should have known that Rudy York would not comply with his orders or show Officer Gray any respect. Up to this point, the only offense was jaywalking, merely a traffic infraction. What he should have done was say something like, "Do me a favor, guys, and please walk on the sidewalk." That probably would have solved the problem.

The Second Contact—When Officer Gray Backed up His Car

Officer Gray gave his order, started to drive away, and apparently thought Rudy York and Johnny Pesky were not obeying his harsh command quickly enough. Officer Gray's actions were reckless from this point on. He could easily enough have gone up the street and let them comply. Instead, Officer Gray traveled a short distance, then put the car in reverse and backed up so that Rudy York and Johnny Pesky were on the driver's side of the patrol car, a tactical mistake. He should have gone up the street to give them time to comply. If they did not, then he could then turn around and put the car between himself and the two men. His position ended up placing the car so close to Rudy York that he could not open his door. Obviously, Officer Gray was not thinking clearly, and he was upset that they did not immediately obey him.

The Third Contact—Grabbing Rudy York through the Door or Window

The accounts of Johnny Pesky and Officer Gray, as well as the evidence collected, differ. Officer Gray stated that he tried to get out of his patrol car; however, Rudy York would not let him open the door far enough to get out. There is no DNA or fingerprint evidence on the outside of the car door to support that York did anything to prevent Officer Gray from trying to exit his patrol car.

Officer Gray's conduct then exceeded the use-of-force continuum when he grabbed York by his throat. This was a complete misuse of force. His action simply escalated the incident well beyond any use-of-force continuum. Up to this point, all that York had done was jaywalk, and all this deserved would be a traffic citation for jaywalking. Anyone reading the department's Use of Force Manual would know that this offense did not rise to any use of force on the force continuum. The most Officer Gray could have been permitted to use would be forceful verbal commands to de-escalate the situation. Officer Gray did not have the legal right to arrest Rudy and, at this point, he should never have placed his hands on York.

Fourth Contact—The Shot Fired Inside the Patrol Car

The evidence is clear that Officer Gray was being assaulted by York inside the patrol car, after York was grabbed. Because Officer Gray was using force that was not legally authorized, York was permitted to use force to prevent an unlawful arrest. If Officer Gray at this time feared for his life or feared serious bodily harm, he had a right to use force, up to and including deadly force. But, he was still holding Rudy York, preventing him from backing away to a safe distance. Officer Gray created a situation for himself where the use of deadly force was the only option, something he should not be rewarded for. He could simply have simply let Rudy York go. He should not have fired his weapon while inside the patrol car.

Fifth Contact—The Shots Fired Outside of the Patrol Car

Officers are trained to fire their weapons when use of force is justified within the use-of-force continuum and doing so will stop the threat. Once the threat is over, officers must stop or reduce their use of force. Here, the use of force was not justified at all. It was 100 percent unnecessary. Once York separated from Officer Gray and started running away, all use of force should have stopped. York ran away from Officer Gray and stopped only when commanded to do so. He complied. At that point, all use of force must stop. York followed directions. He stopped running, he turned around in response to police orders, and he put his hands up. Officer Gray failed to note in his report that York was following instructions. But even if we accept Officer Gray's report, it stated that when York was walking toward him, York was a significant distance away; this is supported because the forensics report did not find any gunshot residue on York's clothing. Officers are taught that a threat can close in and attack from eighteen feet before a shot can be fired by an officer. But here, the evidence shows that York was thirty or more feet away.

In my expert opinion, it is this kind of officer conduct that understandably not only fires up citizens and community groups to seek justifiable prosecutions, but also causes protests and riots. Officer Gray was not legally permitted to fire his weapon. He should have sought cover while waiting for backup. This would have prevented another officer shooting death.

I read with some amazement Officer Gray's Internal Affairs record that he has no prior citizen complaints, and he had not used a firearm in any case before this incident. It is a shame that after five years, he failed to remember what he was taught by me in the Academy. Had he done so, Rudy York would be alive today.

Birdie Tebbetts
_____
Captain Birdie Tebbetts

DARROW COUNTY SHERIFF'S OFFICE CRIME LAB

FILE NUMBER:	CC#YR-1-084395
SUSPECT:	Nita City Police Officer Darren Gray
VICTIM:	Rudy York
SUSPECT:	Officer Darren Gray
LOCATION:	3000 block of Cranfield Drive
	Nita City, Nita
OFFENSE:	CC 187—Murder
DATE OF REPORT:	August 19, YR-1
BY:	Forensic Scientist Whitney Moses

Examination of the Scene

On August 9, YR-1, at about 1045 hours, I heard a Nita City radio call concerning an officer shooting in the 3000 Cranfield Drive area of Nita City, where the victim was lying dead in the middle of the street. Police dispatch indicated that police officers had been dispatched, including Nita City Police Detective Sergeant Goodman, and I heard that there was evidence in the street, including shell casings, blood, possible fingerprints, and DNA samples. Pursuant to our procedure agreement with the Nita City Police Department, I immediately left my laboratory and drove to the location. I arrived at 1118 hours. I could see a number of people in and around the scene where the victim's body was located on Cranfield Drive. In addition to Sergeant Goodman, there was another officer, Officer Gringsty, who was in the process of taping off the scene to contain not only the body of the victim, Rudy York, covered with a white blanket, but also bullet casings, items of clothing, and possibly blood spots. I also observed a white police patrol vehicle with the driver's door open. I initially spoke with Sergeant Goodman, and we agreed that he would conclude his inspection of the scene and then the two of us would take custody of any relevant evidence and ensure that there was no contamination of the evidence and use protective envelopes; I would retain the evidence and process all items for possible laboratory testing, including examining for fingerprints, possible DNA evidence, gun powder residue, and a complete examination of the weapon used by Officer Darren Gray. I am attaching reports on the results of my tests to this report.

Evidence Collection and Preservation

I fully examined Officer Gray's patrol vehicle. First, I tested both the exterior and interior for fingerprints and recovered many prints. I then examined both the exterior and interior for DNA by swabbing surface areas. This evidence was then collected and preserved by me.

We examined the scene for evidence related to Officer Gray's discharging his firearm. Sergeant Goodman then handed over to me Officer Gray's duty belt and firearm, which I placed in a single evidence bag. Then as Sergeant Goodman and I closely inspected the roadway for live rounds and shell casings, I collected and placed them in separate evidence bags.

I followed the medical examiner to his office. There, I recovered York's clothes, placed them in a large protective bag, and transported all this evidence to our lab, where I followed our lab procedures ensuring that we had a complete chain of custody without any others having access to these evidentiary items.

Results of Examination of Officer Gray's Vehicle

- Exterior of the car—In examining Officer Gray's vehicle, I found no evidence from the exterior of the car showing that York had contact with the car. There is no evidence one way or the other that contact was made.

- Interior of the car—DNA evidence was recovered from the driver's inside door panel that, upon analysis, matched Rudy York's DNA. This shows that at some time, some part of his body contacted the door panel. There were no fingerprints from the interior of the patrol car.

Results of Examination of Officer Gray's Duty Belt and Firearm

- The duty belt and firearm were tested for DNA. Both items of Officer Gray contained his DNA in multiple locations: the duty belt, and the hammer and slide of the firearm.

- DNA evidence on the firearm was compared with York's known DNA. The results were inconclusive. In other words, we cannot determine if the DNA came from York.

Results of GFR Examination of Rudy York's Clothing and Skin

The presence of gunfire residue (GFR) is dependent on the distance between the victim and the weapon at the time of the shooting. Analysis must take multiple factors into consideration: the type of weapon fired; the length of time between the shooting and performance of the test, as GFR evidence deteriorates over time; and environmental conditions. The ability to test the distance is not exact; however, there are predictable distances GFR may travel.

- I conducted a GFR test on York's clothing and found lead residue. There was no other GFR component on his clothing, leading me to conclude that York was at a minimum eighteen feet away from the firearm and more probably at a distance up to thirty feet away.

- I did not conduct a GFR test on York's skin. Though gunfire residue is detectable on clothing and skin. I did not test York's skin for GFR because I did not have a GFR kit with me when I first went to the Medical Examiner's Office.

DARROW COUNTY
SHERRIF'S
DEPARTMENT
Crime Laboratory

YR-1-0821
CC#YR-1-084395

DNA Analysis Report
Date Prepared: August 19, YR-1

To: Detective Sgt. Billy Goodman
Unit: SD/DDU
Offense: Homicide

CC#: 14-084395
Biology#: B14-0821
Victim: Rudy York

The following samples were received for DNA analysis.

1- **(C) Buccal Swab** – Rudy York	Property#	12028331.1V1A
2- **(D) Buccal Swab** – Darren Gray	Property#	12028332.1DlA
3- **(E) Swab** – Service Revolver	Property#	12028337.1G1A
4- **(F) Swab** – Driver Door Panel	Property#	12028372.1G9B

The DNA profiles reported were determined by procedures, which have been validated according to the Federal Bureau of Investigation's Quality Assurance Standards for Forensic DNA Testing Laboratories. Polymerase Chain Reaction (PCR) testing was performed using DNA extracts isolated from the items listed above. The short tandem repeat (STR) loci D3S1358, TH01, D21S11, DI8S51, Penta E, D5S818, D13S317, D7S820, D16S539, CSF1PO, Penta D, vWA, DS1179, TPOX, FGA, and amelogenin (gender indicator) were tested and the following conclusions are based on the data.

Sample #1:
Buccal Swab from Property# **12028331.1V1A** yielded a single source profile. The DNA identity of Rudy York is the source of this profile[1].

Sample #2:
Buccal Swab from Property# **12028332.1DlA** yielded a single source profile. The DNA identity of Darren Gray is the source of this profile[1].

Sample #3:
Swab from Service revolver, Property# **12028337.1G1A,** yielded a multiple source profile. The DNA identity of Darren Gray is the source of this profile[1]. Other minor indeterminate contributors are possible comparison to DNA profile of Rudy York, Property# 12028331.1V1A rendered inconclusive results.

Sample #4:
Swab from Driver Door Panel Property# **12028372.1G9B** yielded a single source profile. The DNA identity of Rudy York is the source of this profile[1]. DNA profile of Darren Gray, Property# **12028332.1A.l-2,** can be excluded as a contributor to this profile.

The above evidence samples have been retained in the Trace/Biology Unit. The DNA extracted from the portion of the samples used in this test will be retained as required by Subtitle 2, Section 8-201 of the Annotated Code of Midlands.

Whitney Moses
– DNA Examiner

---

[1] Based on an estimated US population of approximately 330 million (330,000,000) people, random match probabilities of greater than in 330 billion (330,000,000,000) will show at least a 99.9% confidence that the profile is unique in the population.

LOCI	RUDY YORK BUCCAL SWAB PROPERTY# 12028331.1V1A	PROPERTY# 1205732874.1A Revolver Slide & Hammer	Property# 12028372.1G9B Driver Door Panel
CSF1PO	15, 17	7, 9, 15	15, 17, 20
FGA	11, 12	12	11, 12
TH01	6, 8	6, --	6, 8, 9
TPOX	6, 8	8, --	6, 8
VWA	10, 11	10, 11, 32, 34	10
D3S1358	18, 22	20, 24, 29	18, 22
D5S818	30, 30	19, 20	30
D7S820	12, 14	14, 16	12, 15
D8S1179	11, 22	24	11, 22
D13S317	28, 31	18, 30	19, 31
D16S539	9, 13	9, 13, 14	9, 13, 14, 17
D18S51	12, 12	12, 20, 22	12, 13
D21S11	7, 24	11, 19, 29	7, 24
	Comparison	Inconclusive	Conclusive - Match

LOCI	DARREN GRAY BUCCAL SWAB PROPERTY# 12028332.1A.l-2	PROPERTY# 1205732874.1A Revolver Slide & Hammer	Property# 12028372.1G9B Driver Door Panel
CSF1PO	7, 9	7, 9, 15	15, 17, 20
FGA	12, 13	12	11, 12
TH01	6, 7	6, --	6, 8, 9
TPOX	8, 8	8, --	6, 8
VWA	11, 34	10, 11, 32, 34	10
D3S1358	20, 24	20, 24, 29	18, 22
D5S818	19, 20	19, 20	30
D7S820	14, 16	14, 16	12, 15
D8S1179	24, 24	24	11, 22
D13S317	18, 30	18, 30	19, 31
D16S539	9, 15	9, 13, 14	9, 13, 14, 17
D18S51	20, 22	12, 20, 22	12, 13
D21S11	19, 29	11, 19, 29	7, 24
	Comparison	Conclusive - Match	Conclusive - No Match

Preliminary Hearing Testimony

PRELIMINARY HEARING TESTIMONY OF JOHNNY PESKY[1]

1   **Direct Examination**

2

3   My name is Johnny Pesky. I am twenty-two years old, and I live in Nita City. I am here testifying

4   of my own free will and on my attorney's advice. My attorney is present in the courtroom, and

5   I understand that if I need my attorney's advice at any time I can talk with my attorney. I have

6   been told by the District Attorney's Office that I am not facing criminal charges.

7

8   I met Big Rudy about the fifth month after I moved in my two-bedroom apartment. Everyone

9   called him Big Rudy, not Rudy. I had a roommate. I had recently lost my job around the

10   sixth month, but I was on the verge of finding new work and finding a way to pay the bills. So,

11   I was not able to connect with him on a daily basis. He did not live in that same apartment

12   building. He stayed in the Northwinds apartment complex behind my Cranfield Apartment

13   building. I knew him a little over a month before the shooting. I was twenty-two, he was

14   eighteen. I was as comfortable with him as I was when I was with my relatives. He was never

15   a threat to anyone I know, but I didn't hang out with him.

16

17   On August 8, the day of the shooting, I left in the morning around seven o'clock to get cigarillos

18   and something to eat at the store, and I saw Big Rudy across the parking lot. He was putting

19   some kids in a car. I stopped and spoke to him and told him I was going to get some "rillos" and

20   something to eat. He told me he had some weed and said he would match me one. I smoke

21   marijuana in the mornings to start my day off. By "matching," I mean I will roll the weed and

22   he will roll the blunt, and we will exchange the blunts and smoke together. Big Rudy said he

23   would go to the store with me.

24

25   On the way, we stopped because Big Rudy wanted to talk to some construction workers.

26   We walked toward the store on Florissant Street, and when we got there, we saw that it was

---

1. The transcript of Johnny Pesky's testimony was excerpted so that only Johnny Pesky's answers are reprinted here. Assume that this is a true and accurate rendering of Johnny Pesky's answers. The testimony was given at the preliminary hearing on September 28, YR-1, in the Darrow County Municipal Court, Nita City, Nita.

1   closed. There was a sign on the door saying the store would open at 10:00 a.m. Big Rudy

2   seemed annoyed, so we started back to our apartments. Based on what I saw of Big Rudy that

3   morning, it did not look like he had smoked anything that morning.

4

5   We walked back and got to Cranfield, and a police cruiser passed by us and went to McDonald's

6   and parked. We continued on and walked East on Cranfield on the sidewalk, and I saw another

7   police cruiser pass us by. There were not a lot of cars out on Cranfield. This was about 11:30 or

8   noon. We were near the leasing center at the beginning of Cranfield. We were talking about

9   future goals and plans. He asked me how I went from my background to being able to have my

10   own apartment. I told him about the changes I made in my life, about the old days when there

11   were violent gangs and bad stuff all the time. I told him I went to school and was still working

12   on my education. The whole time, there was no traffic on Cranfield, and we were then walking

13   in the middle of the street.

14

15   I was in front of Big Rudy and he was right behind me. We had been doing this for about thirty

16   seconds. There was new traffic, but no one beeped any horns or had to turn their cars away

17   or yelled at us. No more than two or three cars passed us. We were just headed back to our

18   place. As we walked up the street, I saw a police cruiser approaching us coming west toward

19   West Florissant. It was Officer Gray. He got right directly on the side of us, he rolled down his

20   window, and he told us in a rude manner to get on the sidewalk. The words he used were,

21   "Get the fuck on the sidewalk." Big Rudy didn't say anything. I was the one who talked, and

22   I told the officer that we were only a minute away from our homes. I said I live on Cranfield

23   and we'll be off the street shortly. I wasn't loud at all. I just believed that he was pulling off, so

24   we continued to walk, and I assumed that he thought we were just kids and we would get out

25   of the street soon.

26

27   We continued walking and talking, and then seconds later we heard screeching tires and saw

28   Officer Gray's cruiser backing up and it almost struck us. Now we were inches away from

29   his front door. The officer was facing us, and he was talking to us in an angry manner. Big

30   Rudy never said anything to begin with, but at the end of the officer talking Big Rudy said

1   something and suddenly the officer thrust his door open really hard and it hit Big Rudy and

2   hit me on my left side. The officer's left arm was out of the window and he grabbed Big Rudy's

3   shirt around his neck area. I was standing next to Big Rudy on his right side when this hap-

4   pened. The whole thing became a tug of war, with Big Rudy's one hand on the top of the car

5   and the other one on the driver's side mirror trying to get away from the officer grabbing Big

6   Rudy's throat. They were angry—yelling and cussing. I was in shock and couldn't say anything

7   to calm them down. The officer was only using his left arm, so Big Rudy was beginning to pull

8   away from the officer. By this time, three cars could not pass us on Cranfield Drive and they

9   were backed up. I never once saw Big Rudy's hands or body get inside the officer's car. The car

10 was moving and shaking a bit throughout this struggle. This whole thing took place outside

11 the leasing office, which is real close to my apartment and maybe about twenty or thirty feet

12 from Big Rudy's building.

13

14 At this point, I heard the officer say, "I'll shoot." I first thought he meant that he would shoot

15 Big Rudy with a Taser. I looked at the officer and instead of a Taser, he had out his gun. I was so

16 afraid that I couldn't talk. By this time, Big Rudy's left hand is off the top of the car, but his right

17 hand is still in the driver's window because the officer had pulled that hand in the car. The

18 officer started to say something, and at that time the gun went off. Big Rudy was outside the

19 car and the bullet struck him, and I saw blood coming out of him down his right side. I'm not

20 sure whether it was coming from his chest or some other place. I never saw Big Rudy touch

21 the gun or punch the officer.

22

23 I was so scared that I turned and ran as fast as I could. Big Rudy was running behind me. I ran

24 to a small parked car and stood behind it. At that time, the officer was still in the police cruiser.

25 Big Rudy ran by me and told me to keep running. I saw the officer getting out of his car. I stayed

26 there. I then saw the officer walking toward where Big Rudy ran, and he had his gun in his

27 hand. He walked right past me.

28

29 At this point, I was behind the officer and could see his back, and Big Rudy's back beyond the

30 officer. I could see Big Rudy running to a third car, and then I heard the officer fire another

1   shot. I could not tell whether it hit Big Rudy, but I saw him jerk and he suddenly stopped

2   running. Big Rudy was running with his arms down, and as soon as the shot was fired he made

3   a jerking motion and he stopped, turned around, and then he was face-to-face with the of-

4   ficer. The officer was past the last car, and Big Rudy was off the sidewalk and on the street. His

5   hands were up somewhat, one higher than the other because he had already been hit, but

6   they were never near his waist. As I said before, I thought he had been shot. Big Rudy looked

7   like he was trying to say something, but before he could say anything, several more shots fol-

8   lowed. He was able to say, "I don't have a gun," and then the shots were fired. He had his hand

9   up to show the officer that he didn't have a gun. After he was shot that time, when he turned

10 around, he did not take steps toward the officer or maybe a step just to say, "I don't have a

11 gun," or something like that, and he certainly never walked twenty feet toward the officer.

12 It was immediately bang, bang, bang and he fell to the ground. He never got a chance to walk

13 toward the officer, because when he was shot, he fell and never got up. He died right there in

14 the street.

15

16 After this officer killed my friend, he never looked around. He just stood there. I thought now

17 he may come to me. I took off running to save my life. My apartment was close, and the whole

18 time I was hyperventilating and throwing up. I left the apartment soon after and went outside.

19 I could see Big Rudy's body was still lying in the street. There were a lot of people from the

20 neighborhood outside. Nothing stopped people from walking right up to his body. There was

21 a bunch of kids standing right there. People were taking their phones out and taking pictures

22 of his body. I saw the officer's car there, but I didn't see the officer. There was no tape around

23 the scene. I had changed my clothes so the officer would not recognize me, because I thought

24 he might attack me. Finally an officer, not Officer Gray, came to the scene and started putting

25 up tape while Big Rudy's family was trying to find out what happened to him. The officer told

26 them that she did not know and asked them to step back so she could finish taping the scene.

27 I didn't say anything because I was still scared of the police because I had been with Big Rudy

28 and I ran from the officer. After seeing Big Rudy's family at the scene, I went to his grandmoth-

29 er's house at Northwinds. She had just been released from the hospital. The whole family was

30 there. I told them exactly what I have testified to today.

1   **Cross-Examination**

2

3   I was not a buddy of Big Rudy. I didn't know him really well, but all the times that I had been

4   with him, I never thought that he was a bad guy. I never saw him do anything bad. Yeah, we

5   both smoked marijuana, but that doesn't mean there is anything bad. It's not even a crime,

6   just an infraction.

7

8   It is true that when I was really younger I had a conviction for stealing. It was no big deal. I was

9   walking through the third floor of my high school when I was living in North Highlands in Nita.

10   I was nineteen years old and I had already graduated. I was then a freshman at Highlands

11   Community College, but I used to come back to my high school with several buddies, and we

12   would use the gym. As we were walking down a corridor, I saw one of my friends in front of me

13   pick up a package in front of an office and carry it down to the gym. We were shooting baskets—

14   I mean, basketball—and two police officers came in and told me and my three friends that they

15   were investigating a theft reported by one of the teachers. The guy, Benny, had passed out to us

16   a few energy bars that apparently were in the box that Benny picked up. We all pleaded guilty

17   to a misdemeanor petty theft charge, and we all got a three-year probationary period.

18

19   A couple of days after Big Rudy was killed, the police talked to me at the police station about

20   the fact that my being with Big Rudy might bring a probation violation. I thought that was

21   pretty stupid. My probation was almost over, and it seemed to me that they were trying to get

22   me to say what they wanted to protect the officer. It did bother me, along with my concern

23   that they might charge me for some crime connected with Big Rudy's death. So when the

24   police detective took my statement, he told me what the officer's account was and suggested

25   to me that if the officer was right, I could be charged with a felony for lying to the police. It was

26   for that reason, when I was really scared, that I told them what I thought they wanted to hear.

27

28   Later, I spoke to my attorney and realized that I had to testify truthfully, as I did on direct

29   examination. When I was first interviewed by the police, all I could think about was that it

30   could have been me the cop shot. I didn't trust the detective who was interviewing me. I told

1 the detective what I thought he wanted to hear. So, in my original interview, I told the detec-

2 tive that Big Rudy was running toward the cop and that is why the cop shot him. This is what

3 I told the interviewer, that when the cop pulled up to us, Big Rudy charged the cop as the cop

4 was trying to get out of his car, and Big Rudy tried to grab the gun from the cop while the cop

5 was trapped in his car. This was when Rudy was shot the first time by the cop. I told them that

6 after Rudy was shot the first time, he started to run away from the cop car. Soon after, Big Rudy

7 turned around and started running back toward the cop car. I told them that at this point, the

8 cop had his gun drawn and was yelling at Big Rudy to stop and get down on the ground or he

9 would shoot, and Big Rudy continued to run towards the cop. I told them that he was yelling

10 that he was going to "take it from him," and this is when the cop shot him several times. Rudy

11 fell to the ground and died right there.

12

13 I only gave this statement to the police because I was scared for my own life. I had just seen my

14 friend get shot and didn't want the police to come after me. It is always the same police who

15 patrol our neighborhood, and I thought that if I told the police what really happened they may

16 target me. I didn't want to die like my friend did—for no reason.

17

18 Yes, it is true that several of my buddies called me after my first interview with the officer. Yes,

19 they were upset that a cop killed Big Rudy. No, I don't remember who called. Yes, that was

20 before I talked to my attorney. Today I spoke the truth.

I hereby certify that the foregoing is a true and correct transcription of the testimony of Johnny Pesky on September 28, YR-1, at the preliminary hearing in State v. Gray, *in the Darrow County Municipal Court, Nita City, Nita.*

Certified by:

Culley Rikard

CULLEY RIKARD
Court Reporter

TESTIMONY OF CAPTAIN BIRDIE TEBBETTS[2]

1	**Direct Examination**
2	
3	My name is Birdie Tebbetts. I am a captain with the Nita City Police Department. I have been
4	active in law enforcement for over twenty-nine years. The last eight years, I have been the com-
5	mander of the Education and Training Division for the Nita City Police Department. I currently
6	hold a bachelor's degree from the University of Nita in Criminal Justice, and I have a master's
7	degree from the Johns Hopkins University Police Executive Leadership Program (PELP). I am
8	also a graduate of the FBI National School. Throughout my career, I have been assigned to all
9	areas of the department, including patrol, criminal investigations, and special operations.
10	
11	Prior to starting with the police department, I served five years in the United States Marine
12	Corps. A little more than three of those years, I was assigned to our American embassies over-
13	seas. While I was assigned to the embassy in Tel Aviv, Israel, from YR-33 to YR 31, I trained with
14	the Israeli Army on a fighting technique called Krav Maga. I was able to continue my training
15	and received instructor status in YR-29. Because of that, I was introduced into the Education
16	and Training Division as a use of force instructor. I have since become a Level 3 Expert Black
17	Belt. There are five levels of black belt and a master's level.
18	
19	Over time, I attended certification courses with the FBI, the state police, and other organiza-
20	tions across the United States, and I travel twice a year to Israel for recertification and testing.
21	I am the chair of the Use of Force Committee for the International Chiefs of Police Group
22	(ICPG). I helped develop our department's policy on the use of force and the use of force
23	continuum. As the division commander, it is my responsibility to oversee the training of every
24	police officer on the use of force, which includes anything from de-escalation, seeking cover,
25	talking, open hand, compliance, and come-along techniques to the use of force such as strikes
26	with body parts, batons, takedowns, electric shock, and ultimately the firing of the service

---

2. The transcript of Captain Birdie Tebbetts' testimony was excerpted so that only Captain Birdie Tebbetts' answers are reprinted here. Assume that this is a true and accurate rendering of Captain Birdie Tebbetts' answers. The testimony was given at the preliminary hearing on September 28, YR-1, in the Darrow County Municipal Court, Nita City, Nita.

1   weapon. I am on the department's Shot Team. This is a team comprised of highly trained indi-

2   viduals who review any instance of police use of force to determine if policy and procedures

3   were followed. I am on a statewide team and have been for the past three years.

4

5   The Nita City Police Department trains all of the officers in the NCPD and Darrow County

6   Sheriff's Department, as well as all of the city, town, and municipalities in our county. In short,

7   we train officers from all departments within our county, including Nita City police officers.

8   The training includes use of force and annual recertification in firearms. Our department has

9   a firm statement of the duties and responsibilities of all officers in using force in the course

10 of their duties. Exhibit 7 is a true and correct copy of the Nita City Police Manual: Section 8.0,

11 Use of Force.

12

13 I became involved in this case almost immediately after the incident. On August 9, YR-1, at

14 approximately 1203 hours, the Nita City dispatch supervisor sent a text to my Shot Team

15 alerting us to the police-involved shooting. While Shot Teams are not always dispatched to

16 every use-of-force scene, they are dispatched to every police involved shooting in our county.

17 My team was on call on August 9. I was the Shot Team leader. My team consisted of Sergeant

18 Cooper from the Darrow County Sheriff's Department and Lieutenant Axley White of our

19 department. Lieutenant White was on vacation and unavailable. Sergeant Cooper and I arrived

20 at the scene of the shooting at 1550 hours.

21

22 We observed the activities of Sergeant Goodman, who was working with Crime Laboratory

23 Technician Whitney Moses, and, as I recall it, there was another officer protecting all the

24 evidence and keeping bystanders away from the evidence. The Shot Team does not inter-

25 view witnesses or take any statements. First and foremost, the role of the team is to ensure

26 that the integrity of the crime scene is maintained and to witness the collection of evidence,

27 including the removal of the service weapon from the officer involved as well as reviewing all

28 documentation from the case. That documentation includes, but is not limited to forensic,

29 medical examiner, and police incident reports and witness statements. Our next role is to

30 determine whether the officer's use of force, if any, was justified, unjustified, inconclusive,

1   or demonstrates a need for a change in protocol or training. When making our determina-

2   tion, we review the entire incident from the officer's perspective and consider all of the sur-

3   rounding circumstances as the officer perceived them. We view it this way because case law

4   requires that we consider any shooting based on what the officer knew and was experiencing

5   at the time the use of force was taking place.

6

7   Some use-of-force incidents require officers to go through re-training, or in other cases, like

8   the case we have here, our recommendation is to charge the officer with a crime if the officer

9   failed to adhere to use-of-force protocols. I recommended that Officer Gray face charges

10   because he used force that was greater than necessary for the incident and because he did

11   not follow the use-of-force continuum policy for his department. I would like to explain the

12   reasoning behind my recommendation.

13

14   First, I would like to discuss the initial contact with Rudy York. From the very beginning of

15   this incident, Officer Gray failed to conduct himself in a manner comporting with police

16   procedures—he started the encounter in an adversarial fashion. This escalated the situation

17   right from the beginning. From their first day at the academy, police officers are taught that

18   they are part of the community. Getting respect from citizens starts with respecting them

19   first. Based upon what I learned from Johnny Pesky's statement, Officer Gray should have

20   known that the way he spoke with Rudy York would not achieve compliance, much less garner

21   respect. Jaywalking is a low-level offense that is rarely, if ever, enforced. Simply saying some-

22   thing like, "Do me a favor, guys, and walk on the sidewalk," would have increased the prob-

23   ability of citizen compliance far better than Officer Gray's order to move out of the street.

24   I understand that Officer Gray stated in his police report that he was respectful. However, he

25   did not remember what words he used. Therefore, we relied on Johnny Pesky's statement.

26

27   Next, the second contact was made when Officer Gray backed up his patrol car. Once again,

28   jaywalking is a low-level offense. Once the officer gave his order, he started to drive away.

29   Apparently, York and Pesky were not moving in the right direction quickly enough for Officer

30   Gray. Officer Gray's actions can be described as reckless from this point forward. Instead of

1   going up the street and giving the two young men a chance to comply, Officer Gray traveled

2   a short distance, then put his car in reverse and backed up so that York and Pesky were on

3   the driver's side of the patrol car. That is a tactical mistake. Officer Gray should have gone up

4   the street, giving room and time to comply. Then, if they didn't comply, he could have turned

5   around and put the car between himself and the two men. Instead, Officer Gray placed the car

6   with the driver's side so close to York that the officer could not open his door. This shows that

7   Officer Gray was not thinking clearly and was upset that they did not move quickly enough for

8   his liking.

9

10   In the third contact, Officer Gray grabbed York through the door or window. Here, the stories

11   between Pesky, Officer Gray, and the evidence collected differ. In his written report, Officer

12   Gray stated that he tried to get out of his patrol car; however, York would not let him open the

13   door far enough to get out. There was no DNA or fingerprint evidence on the outside of the

14   car door to support that York did anything to prevent Officer Gray from exiting his patrol car.

15   Officer Gray's action then far exceeded the use-of-force continuum when he grabbed York by

16   or near his throat. This was another tactical error and a complete misuse of force. This action

17   by Officer Gray escalated the incident well beyond any use-of-force continuum. At this point,

18   the most action that should have been taken against Rudy York would have been the issuance

19   of a traffic citation for jaywalking. The level of the offense that I accepted as true did not rise

20   to any use of force on the force continuum. At most, Officer Gray would have been permitted

21   to use forceful verbal commands to de-escalate the situation. To put this simply, Officer Gray

22   did not have the right to arrest Rudy York at this point and should never have placed his hands

23   on York, much less grab him.

24

25   In his fourth contact, Officer Gray fired inside of the patrol car. From the evidence, it is clear

26   Officer Gray was being assaulted by York inside of the patrol car, after York was grabbed. How-

27   ever, because Officer Gray was using force that was not authorized, York was permitted to use

28   force in return to prevent an unlawful arrest. If Officer Gray at this point believed his life was

29   in jeopardy or was in fear of serious bodily harm, he also had a right to use force, up to and

30   including deadly force. The problem here is that Officer Gray was still holding York, preventing

1   him from backing away to a safe distance. Officer Gray created a situation for himself where

2   the use of deadly force was the only option. He cannot, and should not, be rewarded for his

3   lack of judgment or failure to take a lesser tactical approach such as simply letting York go.

4   Because of that, Officer Gray should not have fired his weapon while inside the patrol car.

5

6   The fifth contact involved shots being fired outside of the patrol car. Officers are trained to fire

7   their weapons when use of force is justified within the use-of-force continuum and to do so

8   to stop a threat. Once the threat is over, officers must stop or reduce their use of force. I need

9   to be clear: I do not believe the use of force was justified at all in this situation and the firing

10 of the weapon was 100 percent unnecessary. Keeping that in mind, assuming for a moment

11 that it was justified, once York separated from Officer Gray and started running away, all use

12 of force should have stopped. In this situation, York ran away from Officer Gray and stopped

13 only after being commanded to do so. This is called compliance. When an officer observes a

14 subject complying with the officer's commands, all use of force must stop. By all accounts,

15 York was following directions.

16

17 The next and last contact took place after York stopped running. York turned around, adher-

18 ing to police orders. York put his hands up. Officer Gray failed to note that York was following

19 instructions. Even if we accept the written report filed by Officer Gray stating that York was

20 walking towards the officer, York was a significant distance away. We know this because the

21 forensics report noted a lack of gunshot residue on York's clothing. Officers are taught that

22 a threat can close in and attack from eighteen feet before a shot can be fired by an officer.

23 However, the evidence shows that York was thirty or more feet away. It is in my expert opinion

24 that Officer Gray was not authorized to fire his weapon and should have sought cover while

25 waiting for backup. Had he done so, the outcome would have been completely different.

26

27 **Cross-Examination**

28

29 Yes, I did say I relied on Johnny Pesky's statement more than Officer Gray's statement. Well,

30 I suppose if Officer Gray's statement was more accurate, then I would have to reconsider

1   some of my conclusions. Of course, if Pesky gave a statement that was inconsistent with his

2   testimony at this hearing, then that would raise a credibility issue. If cars were driving down

3   the street that Pesky and Rudy York were walking, then that would create a safety issue that

4   would require Officer Gray to consider the jaywalking more seriously. And, if York and Pesky

5   had been smoking marijuana, then it is possible that they could have been under the influ-

6   ence of marijuana and, if so, that could create a safety issue. Yes, I am aware that Pesky was

7   convicted of stealing someone else's property, but I don't think that is important in this matter.

8

9   No, I did not talk directly to any witnesses. As I said on direct examination, our unit does not

10 interview witnesses. So I don't know if there are fair and honest witnesses who would confirm

11 Officer Gray's statement. And, certainly if there are such witnesses, I would consider their

12 statements before I draw my conclusions. Yes, of course I reviewed the police reports before

13 I formed my opinion. But, as I said, I thoroughly reviewed the forensic report of Whitney

14 Moses of the Sheriff's Crime Lab. Well, if I relied on that report to form my opinion and there

15 appeared to be errors in that report, and if those alleged errors were important, then, of

16 course, I would have to reconsider my opinion.

17

18 Yes, the fact that Officer Gray used physical aggression on Rudy York and would not allow

19 him to escape is important. Yes, I heard that Officer Gray claimed that York was trying to grab

20 Officer Gray's gun. And, if that were the case, then that elevates the danger of this incident.

21 But I saw no evidence of that, nor did Whitney Moses. And, even if that were true, Officer Gray

22 appeared to me to be the aggressor who brought on that self-defense action by York. I did

23 see evidence in the reports that Officer Gray sustained injuries to his head, but that would

24 have been the result of his own unnecessary aggression. And, yes, I am aware that in his five

25 years of service Officer Gray had no citizen complaints and had complimentary letters from

26 twelve citizens.

27

28 I did testify to Rudy York's compliance of Officer Gray's commands, and I did say that he fully

29 complied by holding his hands up. And in no way did he appear to be close to Officer Gray

30 when Officer Gray shot him numerous times. Yes, if those facts were not correct, and if he did

1   continue to approach the officer, and if he did not have his hands up in a surrender motion,

2   and if he continued to walk or run at Officer Gray, then the situation is more dangerous. Yes,

3   I know that there was no evidence from the Coroner's Office of any entry wounds to the back.

4   And I do know that Rudy York weighed 289 pounds and was six feet and five inches tall. And

5   I do know that Officer is shorter in height and far less heavy than Rudy York was.

6

7   (Counsel for the prosecution objected to any questions related to this witness testifying about

8   Dr. Rousey Williams, and the Court overruled the objection with the understanding that for

9   the purpose of this preliminary hearing the Court would not allow testimony about facts in

10   any other cases.)

11

12   You ask if I have heard of Rousey J. Williams. Yes, I have. I believe Dr. Williams is in the business

13   of testifying as an expert in the use of force mostly for the defense side of the case. Dr. Williams

14   had law enforcement experience with the FBI but has not served as a law enforcement officer

15   locally. I seem to recall a case or two several years ago where we disagreed in our opinions,

16   but I cannot remember what case it was. If Dr. Williams disagreed with my opinions, no, that

17   would in no way have any effect on my opinion. Dr. Williams has been largely separate from

18   the work of police officers, who are held to a higher standard than they were in the past days.

I hereby certify that the foregoing is a true and correct transcription of the testimony of Captain Birdie Tebbetts on September 28, YR-1, at the preliminary hearing in State v. Gray, *in the Darrow County Municipal Court, Nita City, Nita.*

Certified by:

Culley Rikard

CULLEY RIKARD
Court Reporter

PRELIMINARY HEARING TESTIMONY OF WHITNEY MOSES[3]

1 **Direct Examination**

2

3 My full name is Whitney Moses. I work for the Darrow County Sheriff's Department Crime

4 Lab as a crime scene technician. I graduated from the University of Southern Nita with a B.S. in

5 police forensics in YR-11. I have completed my studies for a Ph.D. in criminal forensics and am

6 currently writing my thesis on gunfire residue left on clothing. My expected thesis presenta-

7 tion and doctoral appointment is December YR-0. I have been working for the past nine years

8 as a crime scene technician for the Darrow County Sheriff's Office, and the past two years as

9 the director of the Crime Lab. I have received certifications in latent fingerprint collection and

10 analysis, as well as DNA collection and analysis. I have been admitted as an expert in these

11 two areas several hundred times in district, circuit and federal courts in the State of Nita.

12 I have been published at least twelve times in the past two years alone on the collection and

13 analysis of fingerprints and DNA in crime scenes. I have also been the featured speaker at

14 several conferences, including the International Association of Crime Lab Technicians annual

15 conference in Copenhagen, Denmark. I received the highest award possible for my field by the

16 same organization for integrity in the field of forensics. I am also trained on gunfire residue,

17 and as I stated before, this is the basis of my Ph.D. thesis.

18

19 I first became involved in this case after hearing the radio call for a police-involved shooting in

20 Nita City. I know from prior history that cases involving officers are often given to the county

21 to investigate. Because of this, I dispatched myself. I arrived approximately 30 minutes after

22 the shooting. There appeared to be some confusion at the scene. Nita City Police Detective

23 Sergeant Goodman was there, along with another officer who was taping the scene. I was not

24 aware of what they were talking about, but after two hours, my team and I were permitted to

25 start processing the scene. I supervised the forensics gathering for the entire scene and was

---

3. The transcript of Whitney Moses's testimony was excerpted so that only Moses's answers are reprinted here. Assume that this is a true and accurate rendering of Moses's answers. The testimony was given at the preliminary hearing on September 28, YR-1, in the Darrow County Municipal Court, Nita City, Nita.

1   present for the collection of everything by Sergeant Goodman, about which I am testifying.

2   I also conducted all of the analysis of the items to which I am testifying.

3

4   I will first discuss the following items that were processed while at the scene. First, my team

5   tested the interior and exterior of Officer Gray's patrol car for latent fingerprints. Dozens of

6   fingerprints were recovered, and I preserved them for later analysis. We then tested the interior

7   and exterior of Officer Gray's patrol car for the presence of DNA evidence by swabbing the sur-

8   face areas. I collected and preserved this evidence, as well. At the scene, Detective Sergeant

9   Goodman turned over to me Officer Gray's duty belt and weapon, which I placed into a single

10   evidence bag. I collected the shell casings I found on the ground at the scene. I followed the

11   medical examiner to his office and recovered the clothes from Rudy York. During this time,

12   I maintained custody of all of the evidence and transported everything to the crime lab, where

13   it was checked in by me pending processing. I followed all established local protocols.

14

15   Now I will discuss the results of my analyses. There was no evidence recovered from the ex-

16   terior of the car that showing that Rudy York had contact with the car. This does not mean

17   contact was not made, only that there is no evidence that contact was made. As to the interior

18   of the car, DNA evidence was recovered from the driver's inside door panel. The DNA was ana-

19   lyzed, and it was determined the DNA belonged to Rudy York. This does not prove that Rudy

20   York was inside of the patrol car—only that at some point in time, some part of his body made

21   contact with the door panel. No fingerprints were recovered from the interior of the patrol car.

22

23   Officer Gray's duty belt was tested inside of the crime lab for the presence of DNA. We

24   tested all of the items on the duty belt, including the officer's service weapon. DNA evidence

25   belonging to Officer Gray was located on all items on the duty belt. DNA evidence found on

26   the hammer of the service weapon and along the slide yielded a multiple source profile. The

27   DNA evidence found on the service weapon was compared against the DNA profile of Officer

28   Gray, and we were able to conclude there was a match. Officer Gray's DNA was located on the

29   service weapon. We discovered evidence of another, unknown contributor to the DNA profile

30   found on the service weapon. The DNA profile on the service weapon was compared against

1   the DNA profile of Rudy York, but the results were inconclusive. We can conclude neither that

2   York's DNA is included in the DNA profile found on the service revolver nor that his DNA is

3   excluded from the DNA profile found on the service revolver.

4

5   In examining   Rudy York's clothing, I conducted a gunfire residue, or GFR, test. Based on my

6   analysis, I determined lead residue to be on his clothing. Lead is one component in GFR and

7   can travel farther than other residues. The fact that no other component associated with GFR

8   was present shows that Rudy York was at least eighteen feet, and possibly up to thirty feet,

9   away at the time of the shooting. I did not conduct a GFR test on York's skin. Gunfire residue

10   is detectable on clothing and skin. I did not test York's skin for GFR because I did not have a

11   GFR kit with me when I first went to the Medical Examiner's Office. The presence of GFR is

12   dependent on a number of factors: where a person is at the time of the shooting in relation to

13   the weapon; the type of weapon fired; the length of time between the shooting and perfor-

14   mance of the test, as GFR evidence deteriorates over time; and environmental conditions. The

15   ability to test the distance is not an exact science; however, there are normal distances GFR

16   may travel.

17

18   **Cross-Examination**

19

20   Yes, my first action at the scene was to inspect all relevant surfaces of objects touched by

21   both Rudy York and Officer Gray and any other individuals at the scene. I dusted the relevant

22   objects in a manner that would best reveal any prints. Yes, fingerprint powder improperly

23   placed on objects can have an effect on the objects that can leave prints unreadable. No, I am

24   confident that nothing I utilized to dust the prints on any object I examined in this case in any

25   way had such an effect. It is possible to examine objects with ultraviolet reflection techniques,

26   but I did not have that available at the scene.

27

28   I suppose that the fingerprint powder could also have a negative impact on the collection and

29   examination of the DNA of relevant parties to the event, but I am always aware of that dan-

30   ger, and I did nothing that would contaminate the DNA that I retrieved and examined. Yes, as

1   I testified earlier, I did locate and examine the interior panel on the inside of the driver's door

2   and the test positively matched Rudy York's DNA. Sure, that would show that York was close

3   enough to the driver's side that he could have had his hand or some other part of his body or

4   body fluid in contact with that portion of Officer Gray's patrol vehicle. And it is also true that

5   I cannot rule out that the unidentifiable DNA on two areas of Officer Gray's gun was left by

6   Rudy York. Well, when you ask me whether there is proof beyond reasonable doubt that Rudy

7   York was not trying to get Officer Gray's gun, that's a legal question. I am not a judge or a juror.

8

9   Yes, in my examination to determine the distance from Rudy York and Officer Gray when the

10   shots were fired, I referred repeatedly to the test and examination of gunfire residue as GFR.

11   Of course, this is a well-known and respected forensic procedure, and yes, it is accepted and

12   used by thousands of forensic science experts.

I hereby certify that the foregoing is a true and correct transcription of the testimony of Whit-ney Moses on September 28, YR-1, at the preliminary hearing in State v. Gray, *in the Darrow County Municipal Court, Nita City, Nita.*

Certified by:

Culley Rikard

CULLEY RIKARD
Court Reporter

Preliminary Hearing Testimony of Detective Sergeant Billy Goodman[4]

1 **Direct Examination**

2

3 My name is Billy Goodman. I am a detective sergeant with the Nita City Police Department.

4 I have been employed by the department for sixteen years. I served six years in Patrol, two

5 years in Internal Affairs, and eight years in Detectives. During those years, I worked a variety

6 of cases including homicides, robberies, burglaries, other crimes of theft, and crimes against

7 the person, such as assaults, batteries, child molestation, and rapes.

8

9 I participated in the investigation involving the death of Rudy York beginning first on

10 August 9, YR-1. Just after 1300 hours, I received a call from dispatch of an officer shooting

11 involving a homicide in the area of Northwinds apartments on Cranfield Drive. I immediately

12 drove to the scene and saw two uniformed officers, Officer Darren Gray and Officer Renata

13 Gringsty. I also saw what was later shown to me to be the body of Rudy York lying under a

14 white cloth. I also saw a number of bystanders, some of whom seemed very upset. Several

15 yelled that this was just another cop murder of an innocent man. I assisted Officer Gring-

16 sty in preserving evidence and keeping bystanders away by yellow-taping the scene. I then

17 immediately talked with Officer Gray.

18

19 Officer Gray seemed in distress and he looked as if he had suffered injuries to his head. He told

20 me that the dead man had attacked him, had beaten him, and had tried to take Officer Gray's

21 gun from him. He explained that he shot York because after he was beaten, York kept coming

22 after him and ignored all of Officer Gray's commands to stop. He said that the only way he

23 could stop York from killing him was to fire shots, as York was only a few feet away from him.

24 I asked him to explain how the incident began.

---

4. The transcript of Sergeant Billy Goodman's testimony was excerpted so that only Sergeant Goodman's answers are reprinted here. Assume that this is a true and accurate rendering of Sergeant Goodman's answers. The testimony was given at the preliminary hearing on September 28, YR-1, in the Darrow County Municipal Court, Nita City, Nita.

1   He said that York and another man were walking down the middle of the street, Cranfield Drive,

2   and he drove by. He knew that this was a hazard, as cars were also driving the same street, so

3   he asked them in a nice way to get off the street and walk on the sidewalk. The two kept walk-

4   ing in the street, so he backed his car to their location, where he stopped and tried to get out

5   of his car. At that point, he said that York came to the driver's door and would not allow him to

6   open his car door. York reached in and started to punch him in the head and face. He told York

7   several times to back off, and then he realized that York was trying to get his gun, which was

8   on the right side of his body. Officer Gray said he had no other option as this was becoming a

9   life-or-death struggle, so Officer Gray was able to get his gun out and fired one shot.

10

11   At that point, he said York and the other man ran from the car. Officer Gray believed that

12   a felony had occurred and he immediately gave chase on foot. York then stopped, turned

13   around, and began moving rapidly toward him. He said that York at one point appeared to

14   reach for a weapon with one hand and Officer Gray began firing multiple shots until York fell.

15

16   At that point, I felt that Officer Gray must return to headquarters, as he needed medical treat-

17   ment, so I relieved him of his gun, belt, and all of his equipment, all of which I later turned over

18   to crime lab specialist Whitney Moses. Another officer arrived and transported Officer Gray

19   back to headquarters. Exhibit 5 is an accurate photo depicting that gun.

20

21   After talking with Officer Gray, I spoke with Officer Gringsty to determine what she had

22   observed and what she had done before I arrived. She said she had arrived a few minutes

23   before I had and she immediately realized that it was necessary to control the bystanders and

24   preserve any evidence at the scene. She began moving the bystanders back and yellow-taped

25   the scene to protect any important evidence from being destroyed. She had not observed any

26   shootings. She saw the dead man lying in the street, and she looked at him and was sure that

27   he was dead. She explained that before becoming an officer, she was an ER aide at Darrow

28   County Medical Center. She was the one who placed the white blanket on York's body. She also

29   told me that she did not see anyone from the crowd touch any of the shell cartridges or in any

30   way touch the body in the street.

1   Exhibit 1, which is called the Rudy York Shooting Scene, fully accurately illustrates the scene

2   and all of the relevant evidence found there. The scene was in the 2900 block of Cranfield

3   Drive within the Cranfield Green apartment complex. You can see at the eastern end of the

4   complex that the road becomes Windward Court. Next to Canfield Green apartment complex

5   on the eastern side is the Northwinds apartment complex. At the western end of Cranfield

6   Drive, the 3000 block changes to single-family homes. Further west of the homes is the inter-

7   section of West Florissant Avenue and Cranfield Drive. All the while I was examining the scene,

8   I was working with Whitney Moses.

9

10   Looking at Exhibit 1, we examined the white Chevrolet Tahoe labeled Police. You can see

11   it parked at an angle facing north, with its left tire nearly sitting on the double yellow line.

12   All doors and three windows were closed. The driver's window was open, with pieces of

13   broken glass on the ground and in the vehicle. The driver's side mirror seemed bent forward,

14   and I could see what looked like human tissue on the outside of the driver's door. Also, that

15   door was damaged and missing paint. Additionally, I saw what looked like blood on the out-

16   side of the rear driver's side door just above the "Police" decal.

17

18   Next, we examined to the road near the police vehicle. I saw a yellow/black/white bracelet

19   near the front driver's side tire, and I found a baseball cap upside down south of the front

20   driver's side tire. There was broken glass south of the front driver's side door. I found a single

21   spent cartridge casing head stamped "FEDERAL 40 S&W," lying just south of the rear driver's

22   side door. And I saw a single spent cartridge casing head stamped the same along the southern

23   curb, south of the police vehicle. Next, I found a brown bracelet under the vehicle behind the

24   front passenger's side tire.

25

26   Whitney Moses and I then walked southeast on Cranfield Drive from the white Chevrolet

27   Tahoe in the southwest lane of traffic and found a white and black Nike sandal upside down,

28   and the toe faced northwest. Further southeast in the southeast lane near the double yellow

29   line was the matching sandal, positioned right side up facing south.

1   We then examined the site where Rudy York's covered body was lying. And then northwest of the

2   police Tahoe in the northwest lane, we found what looked like blood drops west from Coppercreek

3   Court to the body. West of that location were two more spent "FEDERAL 40 S&W" cartridges in

4   the middle of the road, and south of there were two more spent cartridge casings stamped the

5   same. And west of there was one more spent cartridge casing with the same stamp. South of that

6   cartridge in the grass area between the southeast lane of Cranfield Drive and the sidewalk were

7   four spent casings labeled the same as the others. Then we found, northeast of the body in the

8   northwest lane of Cranfield Drive, an apparent projectile that could well have been fired by the

9   same gun. And lastly, we found, south of the body in the southeast lane on Cranfield Drive east of

10   Caddiefield Road, a spent cartridge casing with the same as the other cartridges we found.

11

12   Around 1400 hours, I called the Medical Examiner's Office and spoke to both Investigator

13   Delgado and forensic pathologist Dr. Louis Bader. I asked that they come to the scene, and

14   around 1430 hours they arrived and I explained what I had learned about the shooting.

15   I showed them Rudy York's body, and they conducted their investigation in my presence. I saw

16   Investigator Delgado remove the white cover, then remove identification from the back pants

17   pocket of the body. York's body was face down. He was dressed in a light gray t-shirt, blue

18   underwear, khaki shorts, and a black belt. He had tall yellow socks, with what looked like a

19   pattern of marijuana leaves on each sock.

20

21   I saw what looked like blood on the roadway near York's head. His left arm was bent, and both

22   hands were empty. I saw no weapons on his body or near it. Investigator Delgado moved the

23   body, turning York onto his back. I could see visible gunshot wounds to his right hand, right

24   arm, head, and left forearm. Investigator Delgado removed two five-dollar bills, a notepad, a

25   red lighter, and a black lighter from his clothing, all of which were placed in an evidence bag.

26   They then placed the body in a transportation bag and transported the body to the Darrow

27   County Medical Examiner's Office.

28

29   In my handling of the evidence, I took photos of the scene of Officer's Chevrolet Tahoe,

30   Exhibits 2 and 3, the body on the street, Exhibit 4, and Exhibit 5, the weapon that Officer Gray

1 told me he used to shoot Rudy York. I directed Officer Gray to leave his weapon with me, and

2 he turned it over to me. I later turned it over to Whitney Moses. No one else in my presence

3 handled that weapon. Throughout my scene investigation, I made sure that the only people

4 at the scene who touched evidentiary items were forensic experts from the Darrow County

5 Crime Lab and from the Medical Examiner's Office. All of the items Whitney Moses examined

6 were booked and examined solely by Whitney Moses.

7

8 One of the frustrations I experienced in our investigation was our inability to find witnesses to

9 the shooting. Obviously, the person with York witnessed the entire event. But on August 9, he

10 was nowhere to be found. We canvassed the area and were unable to locate any people who

11 were in a position to see the event from beginning to end. We found a number of tenants in the

12 apartments who heard the shots, but they were either unable or unwilling to come forward.

13 Later, after the protests began, people said they saw Officer Gray shoot Rudy York many times

14 while York had his back to Officer Gray, and many who said that throughout the shootings York

15 had his hands up when he was trying to surrender. Unfortunately, we didn't find any corrobora-

16 tion of those accounts. That is why Johnny Pesky is the only eyewitness we can present.

17

18 As to other evidence that we looked for, I examined an apartment building at 2960 Cranfield

19 Drive and saw damage on the north side of the building. This damage to the vinyl siding above

20 a window on the east side might have been from a projectile. I tried unsuccessfully to extract a

21 projectile, but ceased my efforts because the building was under construction and my extrac-

22 tion would have damaged the building. Also, I checked with apartment complex managers and

23 security companies and learned that no security cameras were present or operated within the

24 apartment complex.

25

26 I continued investigating the case and met with members of our management team. In the

27 process, I met with Johnny Pesky and took an initial statement from him. At the time, for some

28 reason, Pesky seemed to feel that he might be arrested. I assured him that we were not seek-

29 ing his prosecution. Following our initial contact, I met with him again, and he gave us a full

30 and complete statement.

1   **Cross-Examination**

2

3   While I didn't say anything about our department's concern about safety and the protest

4   movement about this case, it was because I was not asked about those matters. I have simply

5   answered the questions that I have been asked. Yes, certainly, that has been a matter of con-

6   cern. It is true that we have met many times and discussed the matter, and we experienced

7   expanded overtime costs and questions about public safety. I recognize Exhibit 6 as a photo

8   depicting one of the demonstrations that took place about two days after the shooting.

9

10   I cannot tell you what was said between Captain Tebbetts and any other members of our

11   department. I have not discussed any matter with Captain Tebbetts. And, no, I have not dis-

12   cussed with anyone in my department anything about the political impact if we did not prose-

13   cute Officer Gray. It is true that Captain Tebbetts did come to the scene after I arrived. I simply

14   explained to the captain what had happened, what I was doing, and what I was going to do.

15   In no way did Captain Tebbetts interfere in my investigation. Certainly, I know what the Shot

16   Team does, and for whatever importance it has, I have great respect for Captain Tebbetts and

17   what that unit does.

18

19   (**COURT:** The record will reflect that the Court has denied the objection of the Prosecution

20   that the following is beyond the scope of the direct examination, and in any case the Defense

21   would be permitted to call this witness and be allowed to ask leading questions.)

22

23   Yes, it is true that Johnny Pesky originally gave me a different account of the incident that

24   led to the shooting. He said that York "charged the cop as the cop was trying to get out of his

25   car." He said that York tried to get the cop's gun while the cop was trapped in his car. And he

26   did say that York turned around and ran back toward the car, and yelling at the cop, and that

27   is when the cop fired his gun. And, yes, when I asked him to show the distance from the cop

28   when he fell to the ground, he indicated a distance in my office that I measured as fourteen

29   and one-half feet. And in looking at Exhibit 1, it does appear that the some of the cartridges

30   appear close to Rudy York's body. But, you have to remember that, at that time, he thought

1 he was going to be arrested when, in fact, he did not break any law. He later corrected this by

2 testifying under oath today what he believed was the truth. It is true that more than once he

3 mentioned his concern about friends and family of Rudy York, and he then gave his second

4 account after our promise that he would not be arrested.

5

6 No, I did not talk to any of Johnny's friends to see if they had called Johnny or to see if any of

7 them had coerced him to change his factual account.

8

9 Yes, we knew that Johnny was a convicted thief. Yes, I have heard the phrase, "You show me

10 a thief and I'll show you a liar." I certainly don't believe that applies to all people, and I don't

11 believe that applies to Johnny Pesky.

I hereby certify that the foregoing is a true and correct transcription of the testimony of Detective Sergeant Billy Goodman on September 28, YR-1, at the preliminary hearing in State v. Gray, *in the Darrow County Municipal Court, Nita City, Nita.*

Certified by:

Culley Rikard

CULLEY RIKARD
Court Reporter

Preliminary Hearing Testimony of Officer Darren Gray[5]

1   **Direct Examination**

2

3   My name is Darren Gray, and I am a police officer for the Nita City Police Department assigned to

4   patrol duties. I have discussed my self-incrimination rights with my attorney before appearing

5   at this preliminary hearing. I understand that I cannot be compelled to testify in this hearing,

6   and I am waving those rights because I believe it is essential that this court hear the full truth

7   of my conduct in the incident in which I am charged with second-degree murder. I am doing

8   this voluntarily.

9

10   I joined the department in October YR-5. Before August 9, YR-1, I had never used my weapon.

11   I have never before been accused of using excessive force. I was not assigned body-recording

12   equipment and was not wearing any on August 9. I have been trained in the police academy

13   in what we call the use-of-force continuum.

14

15   On August 9 of last year around noon, I was on duty working a twelve-hour shift in full uniform

16   in a police car, when I received a call to assist on a sick baby call. I was driving west on the

17   3000 block of Cranfield Drive. The road is one lane each way, separated by a double yellow

18   line, and it has sidewalks on both sides of the street. I saw two men ahead of me walking down

19   the middle of the street causing cars to slow down and drive around them. I had to slow down,

20   and I drove up to them on their right side. I stopped my car and rolled my driver window

21   down. One of the two yelled a few profane words toward me. I said in a normal voice, "Hey,

22   guys, do me a favor and move to the sidewalks." Rudy York, the larger and heavier of the two,

23   yelled at me with a good deal of profanity that they were just going up the streets. They con-

24   tinued walking up the middle of the street. I heard one or both of them yelling and swearing

25   at me that I should mind my own business. I stopped my car, backed up to them to tell them

---

5. The transcript of Officer Darren Gray's testimony was excerpted so that only Officer Gray's answers are reprinted here. Assume that this is a true and accurate rendering of Officer Gray's answers. The testimony was given at the preliminary hearing on September 28, YR-1, in the Darrow County Municipal Court, Nita City, Nita.

1   again to just use the sidewalks. Rudy York walked over to my car, held my driver's side door

2   while yelling and swearing at me, and tried to open the door.

3

4   He moved his body against my car door, all the time yelling something. I tried to push the door

5   open but couldn't do it. Because my window was open, he was able to grab me. I moved away

6   from him, but he reached through the window and started punching me in a wild rage. I wasn't

7   able to push him away with my left hand. He was much bigger and stronger than I was, and he

8   punched me in the head and face. I felt like a five-year-old holding onto Hulk Hogan. I thought

9   I was going to lose consciousness. It seemed to me that he was reaching for my gun. I was lit-

10   erally in fear for my life. I reached for my gun, got it out of my holster, and I yelled to him that

11   I was going to shoot him as he continued to hit me. He yelled, "You're too much of a pussy

12   to shoot me." I believe his hand was still on my gun. I got off one round, he released me, and

13   I fired a second shot. He started running away. At that time, I had no idea who his partner was

14   and where he was. I later learned that he was Johnny Pesky.

15

16   York's attack of an officer and his attempt to get my gun was felonious conduct. I immediately

17   got out of my car and yelled to him to stop running. He was clearly a danger not only to me

18   but to others. I fired several rounds, and he stopped and turned around. I told him to get on

19   the ground. I would say the distance between the two of us was about thirty feet. He did not

20   get on the ground. He raised his arms and yelled to me that he "would take the f****** gun

21   from me." He began walking fast toward me. I told him, "Stop, stop." He then dropped his right

22   arm down, as if reaching for a weapon. He was now about fifteen feet from me, moving right

23   at me. It was like he was going to run through me. I crouched down, and when he was about

24   eight to ten feet from me, I began firing my gun at him. He fell face first to the ground and did

25   not move after that.

26

27   Throughout the whole process, I feared for my life. I only fired my gun when I was in fear

28   for my life. I suffered injuries from the punches to my head. My face was swollen on both

29   the right and left cheeks. I had red marks and scratches on my neck and the hairline, and

30   I received medical treatment. Exhibit 8 is a photo of an area of my right cheek where I was

1   struck repeatedly by Rudy York. As I said earlier, I had never fired a gun while on duty. It was

2   the last resort for me in this case.

3

4   **Cross-Examination**

5

6   I did not have a Taser gun, and generally I don't carry one on duty. I did have a mace canister

7   on my left side, but in no way was I going to pull my left hand away to try and reach it, because

8   my left hand was protecting my face from his punches, and his hands were in front of his face

9   so even if I got my mace, his hands would have protected him. And if any of the mace got on

10   my eyes, I would not be able to see because I wear contacts.

11

12   Yes, I did have an ASP weapon. That device serves several purposes. It serves as a baton. But to

13   reach it, I would have had to lean forward and pull myself to the steering wheel to get it out.

14   I wasn't about to use my good defense hand while he was punching me, and I could not have

15   taken a good swing with it. As to using my flashlight, that was on the passenger side of the car,

16   hard to reach, and it wouldn't do much good anyway.

17

18   Yes, it is true that I did not see Rudy with a weapon, other than the fact was he was trying to

19   reach my gun, and I had to fight him desperately to prevent him from getting my gun. And, no,

20   I didn't see any weapon that he might have had when he was coming at me some to twenty

21   to ten feet away, but I certainly did not know one way or the other whether he had a weapon.

22

23   Yes, I could have stayed in my car and waited for help to arrive, but I had no reason to believe

24   anyone could intervene or protect me as he was coming at me. I had already called for backup.

25   I suppose that I could have driven off before he got to me and waited for assistance, but as

26   I said, this is a man who had tried to get my gun and kill me. I had every legal right and duty to

27   defend myself and apprehend York for felonious conduct.

28

29   I suppose you are right that until I ordered him not to walk in the road, I knew or saw nothing

30   that indicated Rudy had disobeyed any law. Well, maybe it is right that if I had not backed up

1   my car, come alongside of him, and ordered him to move, he would be alive today. But I not

2   only had a right to order him not to walk down the middle of the street, but I had a duty to

3   enforce the vehicle code for his safety and that of other drivers on the road.

4

5   I had blood on my hand and pants after first firing two shots. I assumed that I had hit him once

6   or twice when my gun was first fired, but I certainly did not believe I had in any way stopped

7   him because he was coming at me fast and it was clear that he was going to attack me when I

8   fired the rest of the shots.

9

10   I have read Exhibit 7, the departmental protocol, and I believe that I was following standard

11   police protocol throughout the time from initial contact until I fired the last shot.

12

13   Of course I am aware that Captain Tebbetts is of the opinion that I did not comply with proper

14   protocol. I listened to Captain Tebbetts testify earlier in these proceedings. I was stunned when

15   I heard that Captain Tebbetts would testify against me. I suppose Captain Tebbetts forgot one

16   of the lines that the captain used in training when the captain quoted from a U.S. Supreme

17   Court opinion, "Detached reflection cannot be demanded in the presence of an uplifted knife."

18

19   York had raised his arms and yelled at me, telling me he was going to take my gun away, and

20   I yelled for him to stop, but he kept coming at me faster. He reached down with his right arm

21   as if he was going for a gun, and it was then that I crouched down in a shooting position and

22   began firing my gun and fired until he fell. I then immediately contacted dispatch and fully

23   complied with all orders I received. I cannot believe that any officer under those circumstanc-

24   es would have done differently. I regret that I had to shoot, but I had no other alternative. It's

25   unfortunate, but this was the first time that I fired my gun on duty, and I only did that to save

26   my own life.

27

28   Yes, Exhibit 9 is my official police report. I completed that police report the next day, August

29   10, on orders from my superior officers. They suggested that I could be charged with officer

30   misconduct. I was astonished. I knew that complaints had been made by some community

1   members, but that was the first time I realized that I could be charged with a criminal offense.

2   I said that I understood I had the right to talk with an attorney retained by the police union

3   who represented officers in situations where they could be charged with officer misconduct

4   or criminal charges arising out of police conduct. Up to that point, I had fully answered all of

5   the questions asked of me by my superior officers. I told my superior officers that it would be

6   most helpful if I had the opportunity to review the dispatch records and look at my weapon

7   and photos taken, and I was told that if I did not complete the report immediately, I would be

8   administratively charged with serious officer misconduct.

9

10   I had already talked to every member of the department who asked me to recount the event.

11   I was still experiencing the pain and discomfort of my wounds, and the union attorney told me

12   that I was entitled to have counsel with me. I reluctantly completed that report. In it, I said

13   that I reserved the right to modify the report in the future. I also said that on advice of counsel

14   I would not waive my self-incrimination rights. All I got from them was a scowl.

15

16   You and the court should look at my police record. You will see that I have never received in-

17   ternal complaints from any citizens. In fact, I believe that I have received twelve citizen letters

18   complimenting my police conduct.

I hereby certify that the foregoing is a true and correct transcription of the testimony of Officer Darren Gray on September 28, YR-1, at the preliminary hearing in State v. Gray, *in the Darrow County Municipal Court, Nita City, Nita.*

Certified by:

Culley Rikard

CULLEY RIKARD
Court Reporter

PRELIMINARY HEARING STIPULATION BY BOTH PARTIES THAT THE AUTOPSY REPORT OF DR. BADER BE RECEIVED INTO EVIDENCE

COURT: The record will reflect that counsel for both the prosecution and the defense have stipulated that Exhibit 10, which is attached and set out below, is the autopsy examination report prepared by Dr. Louis Bader, and the court does receive it in evidence in this preliminary examination. Both counsel agree and further stipulate that Dr. Bader is qualified as an expert in performing autopsies and in testifying before the court on the cause of death.

I hereby certify that the foregoing is a true and correct transcription of the court ruling admitting Dr. Bader's autopsy examination report concerning the death of Rudy York on September 28, YR-1, at the preliminary hearing in *State v. Gray*, in the Darrow County Municipal Court, Nita City, Nita.

Certified by:

Culley Rikard

CULLEY RIKARD
Court Reporter

Reports and CVs of Defense Experts

DR. MEL PARNELL
EXPERT DATA
FORENSICS
INVESTIGATOR OF DIGITAL EVIDENCE

995 Professional Drive, Suite 200
Nita City, Nita 11054
(121) 555-6684

November 7, YR-1

Landon Mack, Esq.
Hamner Mack & Schmitz
848 Stock Drive
Nita City, Nita 11058

Re: Client Nita City Police Officer Darren Gray

Dear Mr. Mack:

Thank you again for your referral of Officer Darren Gray's case. As you requested, I have reviewed the case materials which you submitted, and I have enclosed a copy of my curriculum vitae. Those case materials are the transcripts of the testimony of prosecution witnesses Johnny Pesky, Whitney Moses, and Captain Birdie Tebbetts, as well as their reports prepared by the Nita City Police Department and the Darrow County Sheriff's forensic reports. I reviewed the autopsy reports as well. I also reviewed the transcript of the defense testimony of Officer Gray, as well Officer Gray's official police report that he submitted to his department.

I am submitting my expert report summarizing my examination of all the pertinent forensic evidence and reports submitted in this case and outlining the opinions I would express if called to testify as an expert in the upcoming trial of Officer Gray.

As you know, I am an expert and leader in forensics throughout the world. This includes, but is not limited to, crime scene protocols, DNA collection and analysis, fingerprint collection and analysis, and gunshot residue (GSR) collection and analysis. I have my own forensics laboratory, which was established nearly twenty years ago. Before that, I was a police commander in my native country of New Zealand, before immigrating to the United States more than twenty-five years ago. I have analyzed thousands of cases and testified all over the world. I hold three PhDs, each in a different forensic fields. I teach, write, and testify forensics throughout the year. I have traveled the world helping investigate some of the most notorious crimes. I have been admitted as an expert in most of the states in United States including the State of Nita; in state courts as well as federal courts; and have been admitted as an expert in sixteen countries, including Canada, England, Australia, New Zealand, Germany, Belgium, Denmark, Sweden, Poland, and the Czech Republic.

I am being compensated for my time plus expenses, and not for my opinion, as that is not for sale. I dedicate less than 25 percent of my time to my expert qualifications, as I spend most of my time teaching and writing about forensics. I have published in more than fifty journals and a dozen books in the field of forensics. Over the years, I have personally conducted over 2,000 DNA comparisons.

As you know, I became involved in this case two days after the shooting of Rudy York. I was initially asked to participate as an expert bystander in the analysis of the evidence by the Darrow County Sheriff's Department Crime Lab. I was hired by the police union that represents officers of the Nita City Police Department. They were worried that the officer would be tried in the media instead of the courts and wanted to ensure a fair process. The Darrow County District Attorney approved my presence as long as I did not touch anything and remained silent during the forensic examinations. I have since been hired by your defense legal team as a forensics expert for this case.

There are parts of the examination by the crime lab where the crime lab failed to follow proper forensic techniques. In my opinion, the failure of the crime lab to enact these techniques caused the evidence to be tainted and therefore unreliable.

I start with the latent fingerprints on or inside the patrol car. The first test conducted by Whitney Moses was dusting for latent fingerprints. The process of dusting for prints includes the use of a fingerprint powder that attaches itself to largely invisible impressions left by a person's fingerprints. Fingerprint powders, or dust, are a chemical mixture used to bring out prints invisible to the eye. When a technician dusts for fingerprints, he contaminates the entire area with the fingerprint powders, compromising all other types of analysis. The proper method would have been to secure the patrol car and take it to a clean environment. Once there, less intrusive methods should have been used, such as ultraviolet reflection techniques. Had this been done first, fingerprints from anyone in the driver's compartment of the patrol car could have been located. It is in my expert opinion that the use of fingerprint powders in this case compromised the investigation, preventing further fingerprint analysis of the patrol car and one cannot rule out that Rudy York was inside of the patrol car.

As to DNA evidence on or inside the patrol car, contamination of the scene by the fingerprint powder compromised any chance to recover DNA. The crime lab technician stated that this was a conclusive match. However, a cursory review of the crime lab report shows that it is not an exact match with Rudy York's DNA and therefore is completely unreliable. It is in my expert opinion that the lack of DNA evidence inside or outside of the car was caused contamination and does not exclude the possibility that Rudy York was inside the patrol car.

As to the officer's duty belt, the crime lab technician placed the entire duty belt and service weapon in the same evidence bag. Proper protocol would be to place each item into a separate bag. By including all of the items together, steps were not taken that would have precluded cross-contamination or destruction of evidence. It is logical to have obtained DNA evidence belonging to Officer Gray. He wears the duty belt every day he goes to work and would clearly have his DNA on the items. The fact that there was DNA evidence on the hammer and slide of the service weapon and that it was contaminated shows that improper procedures were taken by the crime lab. It is in my expert opinion that if the duty belt and service weapon had been properly separated at the time of collection, the unknown DNA may have been matched and shown a possibility that a second person, including but not limited to Rudy York, had their hand on Officer Gray's service weapon.

It is in my opinion that the gunshot residue testing testimony should not be accepted. Whitney Moses is not certified in this field, and there are several indicators that this person does not have a proper understanding of this type of evidence. In nearly forty years heading my laboratory, I have never heard of "gunfire" residue or "GFR." The mere use of this term instead of "gunshot" residue or "GSR" should give pause to any technician's analysis. The GSR evidence is inconclusive. The fact that GSR was not located on the clothing worn by Rudy York is not unusual, regardless of the distance between Rudy York and the handgun at the time it was fired. Looking at the diagram provided in the autopsy report, only three of the nine shots fired could have struck Rudy York on an area covered by clothing. The crime lab did not collect GSR swabs before Rudy York was removed from the scene. This is Forensics 101 and should have been done at the scene. Even if not at the scene, the test should have been conducted at the Medical Examiner's Office before the clothing was removed. This should have been done even if they were delayed by having to wait for a test kit.

Any analysis of the distance between Officer Gray and Rudy York at the time of the shooting is not reliable and requires additional analysis. Before one can understand GSR fully, one must first understand what a technician should be looking for. A round is a set of components that is placed inside of a weapon and fires a projectile or bullet. The round contains a casing, a primer, powder and a bullet. The casing holds the bullet in place until the primer is struck. This causes a spark that ignites the powder. Once the powder is ignited, an internal combustion within the casing takes place that moves the bullet away from the casing and in the direction the weapon is pointed.

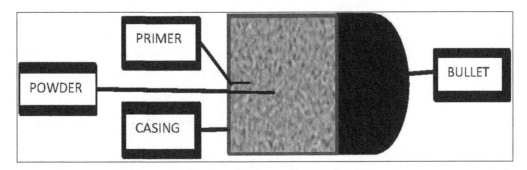

The residue from the powder and the primer igniting is called GSR and may contain burned and unburned parts. Primer and powder elements may consist of lead (Pb), barium (Ba), or antimony (Sb) and may also contain aluminum (Al), sulfur (S), tin (Sn), calcium (Ca), potassium (K), chlorine (Cl), copper (Cu), strontium (Sr), zinc (Zn), titanium (Ti), or silicon (Si). There are other components, of course, with certain powders containing more than twenty-three elements, depending on the individual manufacturer. The importance here is that there are multiple elements present in a proper GSR analysis. Lead residue by itself is often times confused with GSR because it travels along the same trajectory. However, it is considered a separate item because there it does not contain any elements associated with GSR. Any sample containing lead only is not GSR and can only be attributed to the lead bullet. In this case, had a proper GSR been conducted at the scene of the incident to include the skin areas, GSR may have been detected on Rudy York's person. This would have allowed a proper analysis of all of the elements present. Because it was not done, it is impossible to tell how far Rudy York was from Officer Gray at the time he was shot.

Fee Statement

My fee for each day is $4,000. So far, I have provided 6.3 days of service. I have capped my service at ten days, meaning that if I were needed to anything beyond ten days, I would not charge for the additional service. To date, I have devoted eight hours in case review, analysis, and the preparation of this report at the standard rate of $400 per hour, for a total of $3,200. If you require my services as an expert witness in the trial, my fee will be an additional $1,500, plus any travel expenses. If you require additional information or would like to discuss the case further, please feel free to call me.

Sincerely,

Mel Parnell

Dr. Mel Parnell

995 Professional Drive, Suite 200
Nita City, Nita 11054
(121) 555-6684

EDUCATIONAL BACKGROUND

- BA, with Distinction in Forensic Sciences, University of Hawaii, YR-22

- MA, Forensic Sciences, Michigan State University Forensic Science Program, YR-20

- PhD, Forensic Sciences for Firearms, Ammunition, Gunshot Residues and Distance Determinations, Shooting Accidents and Scene Reconstructions, and Ballistic-Related Issues, Nita State University, YR-17

- PhD, Forensic Fingerprint Examination and Identification, Nita State University, YR-15

- PhD, DNA Analysis, Examination, and Identification, Nita State University, YR-13

AREAS OF EXPERTISE

Forensic Expert for:

- Firearms, Ammunition, Firearms Product Liability, Shooting Accidents and Scene Reconstructions, Gunshot Residues and Distance Determinations, and Ballistics-Related issues

- Fingerprint Analysis and Identification

- DNA Analysis, Examination, and Identification

TEACHING EXPERIENCE

- Assistant and Associate Professor of Forensic Sciences, Nita State University, YR-12 to YR-7

- Adjunct Professor of Psychology, Nita State University, YR-7 to present

- Adjunct Professor of Psychology, Nita University, YR-4

- Guest lecturer, Michigan State University, Darrow Community College, Glenback College

FELLOWSHIPS

- Fellow, Academy of Forensic Science Nita University, YR-17

MEMBERSHIPS IN PROFESSIONAL ASSOCIATIONS

- American Academy of Forensic Sciences

- American Association of Forensic Science Examiners

- State of Nita Forensic Association

- International Academy of Forensic Science Examination

CERTIFICATION AND HONORS

- Certified, American Board of Forensic Science Examiners, YR-10

- Distinguished Contribution Award, American Forensics Science Foundation (Gunshot Testimony), YR-9

- Research Award, National Science Foundation (False Fingerprint Analysis), YR-8

- Forensic Expert of the Year, Nita Forensic Association, YR-8

- Excellence in Expert Forensics Award, Nita Criminal Defense Counsel Association, YR-3

PUBLICATIONS

- Parnell, M., *Reliability of Distance Estimation of Gunshots*, Journal of Forensic Firearm Discharge (YR-12)

- Miller, D. E. & Parnell, M., *Expert Examination of Ammunition Identification Reliability*, Journal of Computer Technology (YR-10)

- Parnell, M., *Why are Forensic Proficiency Tests So Lousy?*, Journal on Scientific Evidence (YR-8)

- Casparak, W. & Parnell, M., *What Happens in the Courtroom When an Expert Makes Mistakes?* Constitutional Law Journal (YR-7)

- Parnell, M. & Guzik, E., *Dismal Results Caused by Police Bias*, Academy of Criminal Defense Journal (YR-5)

- Donaldson, W.K. & Parnell, M., *The Gross Inadequacy of Proper Training of Gunshot Expertise: When Will It Change and What is Necessary?* The International Academy of Forensic Science Bulletin (YR-3)

- Parnell, M., *Do Police and Prosecutors Corrupt Eyewitness Identification?* Nita Defense Counsel Quarterly (YR-2)

- Parnell, M., *Is DNA Evidence As Good As It Seems?*, American Association of Trace Evidence Examiners (ASTEE) Monthly, (YR-1)

SELECT PRESENTATIONS

- Instructor, DEA Clandestine Laboratory Safety Certification, Salt Lake City, UT, YR-9

- Instructor, MSP Supervisory Development Program, YR-9

- Instructor, MSP Evidence Technician/ Detective Schools, YR-9

- Instructor, MSP Bloodstain Pattern Analysis Workshops, YR-8

- Chair, MAFS Training & Education Committee, YR-7

- Chair, MAFS Trace Evidence Section, YR-7

- Coordinator, Science Crime Event, MI Science Olympiad, YR-5

- Coordinator/Speaker, MAFS Advanced Trace Evidence Symposium, Nita City, Nita, YR-3

- Moderator, GHB Symposium, American Academy of Forensic Sciences Meeting, Reno, YR-2

REPORT OF ROUSEY J. WILLIAMS

992 Professional Drive
Nita City, Nita 11026
(121) 555-3787
(800) EXPERTS

November 7, YR-1

Landon Mack, Esq.
848 Stock Drive
Nita City, Nita 11058

Re: Officer Darren Gray

Dear Mr. Mack:

In response to your request that I review the investigation reports and the transcripts of testimony in Officer Gray's preliminary hearing, I am setting forth my expert report concerning the use of force employed in this case by Officer Gray and my intended testimony should this case go to trial.

My Background, Training, and Experience

I am the CEO of the Rousey Williams Law Enforcement Expertise firm. My company is located in Nita City, Nita. I am a mixed martial arts international champion and hold a 4th-degree black belt in judo. I graduated from Stanford University with a dual bachelor's and master's degree in justice administration in YR-23. I then attended Pepperdine Law School, where I graduated *summa cum laude* in YR-20. After that, I became an FBI agent and spent most of my career in Washington, D.C. While I was in Washington, I attended a PhD program from John Jay College in New York and received my doctorate in criminal justice in YR-16.

Sometime in YR-15, I was assigned to the Department of Justice and participated on a team designed to investigate civil rights violations by police officers and departments. Over the course of my career with the FBI, I have either testified in trial or provided reports that were used to settle matters in over 250 cases. In all of those cases, I testified or wrote reports that were adversarial to the officer or department. My expertise was in use-of-force standards and application. I retired in YR-5 from the FBI and started my own company. I have twenty-three employees, mostly retired agents, and we investigate use of force incidents around the nation. My company has investigated 127 use-of-force incidents. We determined in 101 of them that the officer or the department was in violation of use-of-force protocols. In the remaining twenty-six cases, we determined that the officer's actions were proper. I testified in all twenty-six cases in state or federal courts throughout the United States. Between my time with the FBI and my time with my company, I have been accepted and testified as an expert a total of seventy-three times. We charge a flat fee for our services which is $10,000 per case, plus expenses. This covers our investigation and report. Any time spent in court is an additional $1,000 per day, plus expenses. I was hired on September 1, YR-1, by your office to review this case. I personally conducted the evaluation of this case and had my team review my findings. I conducted my investigation as a neutral party, letting only the evidence shape my expert opinions.

I began by reviewing the preliminary hearing testimony of all of the witnesses for the prosecution. I reviewed all of the evidence produced in discovery, and I read all of the police reports, witness statements, medical reports, forensic reports, as well as viewing the video tapes. I also personally viewed the area of the incident in Nita City.

The death of Rudy York, a teenager, is a tragedy that demands a full investigation to determine whether someone needs to be held accountable. Based upon all of the evidence presented thus far in this case, it is in my expert opinion that Officer Gray was in fear for his life and acted in accordance with all use-of-force standards. His actions were not only justified, it is my opinion that they were necessary.

The Initial Contact with Rudy York

The easiest way to explain my reasoning is to look at the actions of the officer on the day of the incident, as described by Captain Tebbetts. Taking the stages of the incident as described by Captain Tebbetts, I reviewed the initial contact with Rudy York. Captain Tebbetts takes issue with the manner in which Officer Gray first interacted with York. If true, I agree that Officer Gray did not approach York and Johnny Pesky in an appropriate manner. His dialogue, taken at face value as true was rude and unprofessional. However, that has nothing to do with the use of force in this case. In less serious scenarios, Officer Gray would have been subjected to a behavioral counseling write-up, a low-level type of punishment.

There is no reason to believe Officer Gray was rude or inappropriate. In fact, I reviewed Officer Gray's personnel file and his disciplinary record. In six years of service, Officer Gray has not received a single citizen complaint. This is highly unusual for an officer with six years in any police department. Officer Gray has received twelve letters of appreciation from citizens during his six years. This is remarkable and speaks volumes about this officer. Complaint letters come easy, but he has none; compliment letters are rare, yet he has twelve. Johnny Pesky is the only person who is claiming Officer Gray acted rudely. However, this is completely different from his original statement to police. Moreover, Pesky did not change his statement until after the York family hired an attorney. That attorney then spoke with Pesky before he gave his second statement. Based on the evidence presented, Pesky's statements are not credible and therefore should not have any bearing in this case.

The Second Contact: When Officer Gray Backed Up His Patrol Car

Once again, I agree with Captain Tebbetts to a certain degree, that jaywalking is a low-level offense. However, officers are charged with enforcing the law and Officer Gray was well within his authority to enforce this provision. Officer Gray gave an order, he moved on, and he was ignored. He had a duty to go back and make sure the two people complied with the order. Look at it this way: if these young people had been run over, the officer would have been negligent in his duties if he did not go back. This second contact is not only justified, but necessary.

Captain Tebbetts complains that Officer Gray made a tactical error by backing up his patrol car. In reality, the fact that Officer Gray backed up his car shows Officer Gray's state of mind. Clearly, Captain Tebbetts believed a tactical response was necessary; however, Officer Gray did not perceive a threat and was doing just as he noted in his written report. All he wanted was for the two men to comply. He did not know his life was in danger; therefore, there was no need to make a tactical driving maneuver.

Pesky claimed that Officer Gray drove his car to the sidewalk right up against them. This is clearly not the case, as the patrol car was parked in the travel portion of the roadway. There is no evidence the car was moved after the confrontation. Furthermore, even if Officer Gray drove close to them, this did not provide Pesky or York a legal or reasonable justification for assaulting a police officer.

Lastly, none of this matters. Based on case law, the actions of the officer are supposed to be judged at the time the officer decides to use force. Anything the officer does before that time simply does not matter. In other words, the first and second contacts have no bearing on the officer's use of force. It is my expert opinion that these two contacts are being used to inflame the jury to lay some basis for the charges.

The Third and Fourth Contacts Protecting Himself against an Attack

What happened here is disputed; however, a few things are clear. York struck Officer Gray. His strikes caused Officer Gray to sustain injuries that warranted a trip to the hospital. While nothing was broken, a person can only sustain a few head blows before they become unconscious. Officers are trained to repel attacks and to use force, including deadly force if they are in fear of their life or serious bodily injury. Being hit in the face and head are legitimate concerns for the use of deadly force.

For whatever reason, Officer Gray and York were involved in a physical altercation inside of the patrol car. We know the crime lab failed to follow proper protocol. However, we have Pesky's statement, we have DNA evidence belonging to York from inside the patrol car, and Officer Gray has injuries. Because York and Pesky ran away at some point, the only way the officer could have been injured would have been during a confrontation inside of the patrol car. Because we know Officer Gray was assaulted inside of the patrol car, we also know that Officer Gray's actions were within the use-of-force continuum. He had a right and an obligation to use the force necessary to repel the attack, including the use of deadly force.

The Fifth Contact: When Shots Were Fired Outside The Patrol Car

Once again, I agree with Captain Tebbetts that officers are trained to fire their weapons when the use of force is justified within the use-of-force continuum and to do so to stop the threat. Once the threat is over, officers must stop or reduce their use of force. Captain Tebbetts is also correct that once York ran away from the car, the use of force should have stopped. From all accounts, Officer Gray fired a couple of shots while York had his back turned and then stopped firing. None of these shots struck York. We know this because the medical examiner's report shows us that all of the entrance wounds were to the front portion of York's body. There are a few instances when an officer is permitted to fire at a fleeing felon. In this case, Officer Gray could have been justified in firing those shots, but that is not why we are here. We are here to determine if the remaining nine shots were justified.

At this point in the confrontation, York turned around. Instead of complying with orders to stop, he walked toward Officer Gray. It is very important to understand what the officer knew at the time of the shooting:

- Officer Gray already had a confrontation with York

- York was aggressive and caused injuries to Officer Gray

- York failed to comply with the reasonable orders of a police officer

- York was now approaching Officer Gray

And, according to the first statement from Pesky and the written report of Officer Gray, the use of force that followed was justified because:

- York started running toward Officer Gray

- York most likely had his hands in the air; however, saying that you are giving up and giving up are two different things

- York did not give up

- Instead, he was running toward the officer and yelled that he was going to take the gun away from the officer

- Fearing for his life, Officer Gray used deadly force, firing nine rounds until he perceived the threat had stopped, consistent with his training and the use-of-force continuum

It is clear from the facts of this case that, while not a popular position, the use of force was necessary. There is no requirement for an officer to endure additional punishment and fight for his life before using force. While unpopular, this was the only remaining avenue for this officer to take, and the use of deadly force was absolutely necessary.

Captain Tebbetts notes that York was a significant distance away. First and foremost, we do not know how far York and Officer Gray were from one another because of the bumbling job performed by the crime lab technician. However, we do know from the location of the shell casing and the body of York when he hit the ground, there were fewer than thirty feet between the officer and the victim. Officers are not required to wait until a suspect is within eighteen feet. This distance is the time it will take the average person to close the distance between himself and his target from a standing position. In this situation, York was not average. He was a healthy, eighteen-year-old man with a running head start. Officer Gray would most likely not be alive today if he waited for York to be inside of eighteen feet before firing his first round.

Based on all of the evidence presented, it is in my expert opinion that Officer Gray did the only thing he could do and his use of deadly force was well within the use-of-force continuum. Officer Gray was authorized and well within his right to fire his weapon and do so until the threat stopped.

I would add a little bit of background about Captain Tebbetts's background as an expert and as one who apparently disagrees strongly with my opinion in this case. It is apparent that Captain Tebbetts, as well as others in both the Nita City Police Department and the Darrow County District Attorney's Office have a great concern that there may be severe political damage for their offices and for the future of their leaders if this case is not filed and if a conviction does not result. A segment of the Nita City residents have protested the death of Rudy York and caused the print, television, and radio media to cover this issue daily. It is also unfortunate that they can only produce an in-house expert in use of force by police officers—in this case, someone who I have differed with severely in more than one previous case. Two of those cases proceeded to trial, and in both cases the juries in their findings disagreed with Captain Tebbetts. One was a civil suit for damages, and the other was about five years ago, *State v. DiMaggio*. Officer DiMaggio was acquitted of misdemeanor battery. The jurors, after the trial, were quoted that they were annoyed that the alleged victim should have been prosecuted. I realize that the court will probably disallow this to be raised if Officer Gray's case proceeds to trial.

Rousey J. Williams
_____

Rousey J. Williams, PhD

ROUSEY WILLIAMS

992 Professional Drive
Nita City, Nita 11026
(121) 397-3787
(121) EXPERTS

EDUCATIONAL BACKGROUND

BA and MS in justice administration, Stanford University of Hawaii, YR-23

JD, *summa cum laude*, Pepperdine Law School, YR-20

Ph.D. in criminal justice, John Jay College, YR-16

EMPLOYMENT HISTORY

In YR-19, I joined the FBI as an investigator and was assigned handle civil rights violations in Washington, D.C.

In YR-16, the FBI assigned me to the Department of Justice Civil Rights Team that investigated civil rights violations by police officers and departments. In that capacity, I testified in trial or provided reports that were used to settle matters in over 250 cases. My expertise was in use-of-force standards and application.

In YR-5, I retired from the FBI and formed the Rousey Williams Law Enforcement Expertise firm in Nita City. My firm consists of twenty-three employees, most of whom are former agents. We have investigated 127 use-of-force cases throughout the nation. We determined in 101 of those cases there were violations of use-of-force standards, and in twenty-six cases where I testified, the conduct was proper. I have been accepted and testified as an expert in both state and federal courts.

TEACHING EXPERIENCE

U.S. Department of Justice FBI Law Enforcement Academy, YR-8

American Association of Law Enforcement Examiners, Washington, D.C., YR-5

Nita State University Criminal Justice Department Annual Law Enforcement Address, YR-4

MEMBERSHIPS IN PROFESSIONAL ASSOCIATIONS

Darrow County Law Enforcement Association, Guest Member

American Association of Law Enforcement Instructors

Nita State Criminal Law Experts Foundation

American Academy of Court Justice

National Criminal Defense Association (NCDA)

American Bar Association

Nita State Bar Association

PUBLICATIONS

Williams, R., *The Failure of Law Enforcement Agencies to Adequately Instruct Their Officers; What Will it Take to Change?* The Nita Criminal Defense Association Journal, YR-4

Williams, R., *The Immense Fiscal Damage from Law Enforcement Mistakes*, Nita State Government Leaders Monthly Bulletin, YR-3

Galves, F. & Williams R., *Politics Influence on Criminal Justice*, Nita State Bar Association Journal, YR-2

STATEMENT OF DENNY GALEHOUSE

My full name is Denny Galehouse. I was born on February 14, YR-40. I reside at 101 Cranfield Drive, Nita City. I am currently working for Cranfield apartments as a Maintenance Mechanic III. As part of my salary, I live in one of the units and I am in charge of the maintenance for two of the eight buildings located on Cranfield Drive. I have lived in this neighborhood all of my life.

The neighborhood goes up and down, but it is a good place to live. Good people live here, but we have our share of folks who like to test the boundaries. The police around here tend to treat people as if they are always doing something wrong. We don't see them that often, but when we do, they usually try to mix things up. They leave me alone, but I have seen how they do things around here. They rile people up, then lock them up when they get out of hand. It is a shame, really. Police should care more about the people they are supposed to protect.

I was working on August 9, YR-1. I did not see or hear everything, but I could see most of it. I was coming around the northern building seen on the picture the prosecutor showed me. I was coming from the north, and I marked the picture Exhibit 12 with a capital DG to show where I was standing. I was looking into a complaint of water seeping into the building. I was thinking the mortar needed to be replaced. I was checking out the building when I heard tires making some noise. It was abrupt, so it grabbed my attention and I turned around. A patrol car had just backed up to where two young people were standing. The passenger side of the car was facing me, so I could not see the entire thing.

From the looks of it, one of them was arguing with the officer. I could not hear what they said, but all of a sudden, the young man is inside of the patrol car. You can tell they were fighting or struggling with each other. I have since been shown a picture, and I recognize the person arguing with the officer is Rudy York. The second person was Johnny Pesky. They both live in the apartments and they don't give me any trouble.

All of a sudden, I heard a large boom and Johnny Pesky ran away to the apartment complex and hid down behind some cars. At the same time, Rudy York was running away from the car. I thought the officer was hurt because he did not emerge right away. It took him a moment. Rudy had gotten about forty to fifty feet away when the officer was out of his car screaming. I could not tell what he was saying, but I could hear him screaming. All of a sudden, Rudy stopped running and he turned around, putting his hands up above his head. It seemed like he and the officer were talking to each other as the officer was closing the distance between the two.

Rudy then started walking towards the officer and the officer stopped walking. I could hear him yell, "Stop . . . stop," a couple of times, but Rudy kept coming. It seemed like the officer was yelling for him to get down, but I could not tell exactly what he was saying. I heard him yelling and I saw him pointing to the ground with his left hand. Rudy did not stop and the officer seemed like he got real low, just like I was taught when I was in the service. He started firing his gun. Rudy just kept coming towards the officer and then after what seemed like a dozen shots, he fell to the ground.

The officer froze for a minute, and then you could see him walking up to Rudy. Officer Gray looked at Rudy and then started talking on the radio. It took about another minute for a bunch of police to arrive and another fifteen minutes for an ambulance to get there. They just left Rudy on the street without giving him any first-aid. They all just watched him die. The entire thing took about thirty to forty-five seconds. It was very fast. I am sure it felt like a long time to everyone else, but I am sure how long this took. I keep track of my time all day for the work I do. I am sure it did not take any longer than that.

I would add that I am not a big fan of the police, but in this case it appeared clear to me that Rudy was walking at Officer Gray to attack him and he was approaching fast, and if Officer Gray had not fired the gun, Rudy would have gotten to him.

When I was in the Army, I was part of a unit that handled most of the mechanical functions at our base, so I had a good mechanical background. It is true that I was discharged from the Army about six years ago for using drugs, so I did not have an honorable discharge. About six months later, I got in some trouble when I was arrested for what they called Possession for Sale of Meth, a felony, but they reduced it to Possession of Meth, a misdemeanor, and as a condition of probation I served six months in the Darrow County jail. I have been clean since that arrest. I am now married and have one child. My employer knows about my past, and they have informed me multiple times that they are very happy with my work. They have promoted me twice and given me raises and more responsibility.

Signed: _Denny Galehouse_   Date: 9/20/YR-1

Denny Galehouse

Witnessed by: _Margaret Beach_   Date: *September 20, YR-1*

Investigator Margaret Beach

Arrest and Conviction Records

Arrest and Conviction Record of Rudy Calvin York

RE: BAGBY, J. DDA DATE: 11-11-YR-1 TIME: 1458
CIR/B7653449
NAM/01 YORK, RUDY
NAM/02 YORK, aka BIG RUDY
SOC/535017849

****

ARR/DET/CITE/CONV:
#1
07-08-YR-4 ARREST NCPD CC 11357(b)-POSSESSION OF MARIJUANA, MISDEMEANOR
07-20-YR-4 PETITION SUSTAINED, JUVENILE COURT, WARDSHIP
09-09-YR-4 VIOLATION OF PROBATION, REVOKED, 5 DAYS JUVENILE HALL

****

ARR/DET/CITE/CONV:
#2
07-08-YR-3 ARREST DCSD C.C. 11357(c) POSSESSION OF MORE THAN 28.5 GRAMS OF MARIJUANA, MISDEMEANOR
07-27-YR-3 PETITION SUSTAINED, JUVENILE COURT, INFORMAL SUPERVISION, 1 YEAR PROBATION

****

ARR/DET/CITE/CONV:
#3
11-24-YR-2 ARREST DCSD C.C. 415 DISTURBANCE OF THE PEACE, MISDEMEANOR, & C.C. 647(f), PUBLIC INTOXICATION, MISDEMEANOR
12-12-YR-2 PETITION SUSTAINED, JUVENILE COURT, INFORMAL SUPERVISION, 1 YEAR PROBATION

NOT TO BE DUPLICATED

Arrest and Conviction Record of Johnny Pesky

RE: BAGBY, J. DDA DATE: 11-11-YR-1 TIME: 1515
CIR/D9428731
NAM/01 PESKY, JOHNNY
NDL/M7882929
SOC/25586414

****

ARR/DET/CITE/CONV:
#1
03-13-YR-3 CIT. NDA CC 484-GRAND THEFT, FELONY
04-14-YR-5 PLEA NO CONTEST, CONVICTION, MISDEMEANOR PETTY THEFT CC 487, 3 YEARS PROBATION, 1 YEAR COUNTY JAIL, SUSPENDED, RESTITUTION PURSUANT TO CIVIL JUDGMENT

NOT TO BE DUPLICATED

ARREST AND CONVICTION RECORD OF DENNY GALEHOUSE

RE: BAGBY, J. DDA DATE: 11-11-YR-1 TIME: 1458
CIR/B7653449
NAM/01 GALEHOUSE, DENNY
NAM/02 GALEHOUSE, SARGE
SOC/535017849

****

ARR/DET/CITE/CONV:
#1
03-10-YR-5 ARREST DCSD C.C. 11357(a) POSSESSION FOR SALE OF METHAMPHET-AMINE, FELONY
04-14-YR-5 PLEA NO CONTEST,CONVICTION, MISDEMEANOR CC 11357(b), POSSESSION OF METHAMPHETAMINE, 3 YEARS PROBATION, 1 YEAR COUNTY JAIL, 6 MONTHS SUSPENDED
05-25-YR-2 EXPUNGMENT OF CC 11357(b) CONVICTION PURSUANT TO COURT ORDER UNDER CC 1904 PROBATION SERVED AND COMPLETED

****

NOT TO BE DUPLICATED

Applicable Nita Criminal Code

Nita Criminal Code § 100—Murder

Murder is the unlawful killing of a human being or a fetus with malice aforethought.

Nita Criminal Code § 102—Second-Degree Murder

1) A person commits the crime of second degree murder if:

   a) He or she intentionally, but not after deliberation, causes the death of a person, or

   b) With intent to cause serious bodily injury to a person other than himself or herself, he or she causes the death of that person or of another person

2) Second-degree murder is a felony punishable by confinement in prison for fifteen to fifty years.

Nita Criminal Code § 103—Voluntary Manslaughter

1) A person commits the crime of voluntary manslaughter if he or she intentionally, but not after deliberation, causes the death of a person, under circumstances where the act causing the death was performed upon a sudden heat of passion caused by a serious and highly provoking act of the intended victim, affecting the person killing sufficiently to excite an irresistible passion in a reasonable person. However, if between the provocation and the killing there is an interval sufficient for the voice of reason and humanity to be heard, the killing is murder.

2) Voluntary manslaughter is a felony punishable by confinement in prison for seven to twenty years.

Nita Criminal Code § 104—Criminally Negligent Homicide

1) A person commits the crime of criminally negligent homicide, if:

   a) By conduct amounting to criminal negligence, he or she causes the death of a person; or

   b) He or she intentionally causes the death of a person, but believes in good faith that circumstances exist which would justify the killing, but the belief that such circumstances exist is unreasonable.

2) A person acts with criminal negligence when, through a gross deviation from the standard of care that a reasonable person would exercise, he or she fails to perceive a substantial and unjustifiable risk that a result will occur, or that a circumstance exists.

3) Criminally negligent homicide is a misdemeanor punishable by confinement in the county jail for up to one year, or by a fine of up to $10,000, or both.

Nita Criminal Code § 105–Justifiable Homicide

Homicide is justifiable when committed by any person in any of the following cases:

1) When resisting any attempt to murder any person, or to commit a felony, or to do some great bodily injury upon any person; or,

2) When necessarily committed in attempting, by lawful ways and means, to apprehend any person for any felony committed, or in lawfully suppressing any riot, or in lawfully keeping and preserving the peace.

However, a bare fear of the commission of any of the offenses mentioned in subdivisions 1 and 2 of this section, to prevent which homicide may be lawfully committed, is not sufficient to justify it. But the circumstances must be sufficient to excite the fears of a reasonable person, and the party killing must have acted under the influence of such fears alone.

Nita Criminal Code § 415 – Disturbing the Peace

Any of the following persons shall be punished by imprisonment in the county jail for a period of not more than ninety days, a fine of not more than $400, or both such imprisonment and fine:

a) Any person who unlawfully fights in a public place or challenges another person in a public place to fight.

b) Any person who maliciously and willfully disturbs another person by loud and unreasonable noise.

c) Any person who uses offensive words in a public place which are inherently likely to provoke an immediate violent reaction.

Nita Criminal Code § 487a—Petty Theft

1) Every person who takes, steals, carries or drives away, defrauds another of, or obtains by false or fraudulent representation the personal property of another of a value of $400 or less is guilty of petty theft.

2) Petty theft is a misdemeanor punishable by confinement in the county jail for up to six months, or by a fine of up to $1,000, or by both.

Nita Criminal Code § 647(f)—Public Intoxication

Every person who is found in any public place under the influence of intoxicating liquor, any drug, controlled substance, or any combination of any intoxicating liquor, drug, controlled substance, in a condition that he or she is unable to exercise care for his or her own safety or the safety of others, or by reason of his or her being under the influence of intoxicating liquor, any drug, controlled substance, or any combination of any intoxicating liquor, drug, interferes with or obstructs or prevents the free use of any street, sidewalk, or other public way is guilty of a misdemeanor.

Nita Criminal Code § 11350 – Possession of a Controlled Substance

1) Every person who possesses any controlled substance which is a narcotic or dangerous drug, unless upon the written prescription of a physician, dentist, podiatrist, or veterinarian licensed to practice in this state, is guilty a felony.

2) A violation of this section shall be punished by imprisonment in the state prison.

Nita Criminal Code § 11351—Possession for Sale of Methamphetamine

1) Every person who possesses for sale methamphetamine, or preparation thereof, is guilty of a violation of this section.

2) Possession for sale of methamphetamine is a felony punishable by confinement in prison for three, four, or five years.

Nita Criminal Code § 11357(c)—Possession Marijuana

1) Every person who possesses more than 28.5 grams of marijuana, other than concentrated cannabis, is guilty of a misdemeanor.

2) A violation shall be punished by imprisonment in the county jail for a period of not more than six months or by a fine of not more than $500, or by both such fine and imprisonment.

JURY INSTRUCTIONS

PART I. PRELIMINARY INSTRUCTIONS GIVEN PRIOR TO EVIDENCE

1.01 INTRODUCTION

You have been selected as jurors and have taken an oath to well and truly try this case.

During the progress of the trial, there will be periods of time when the court recesses. During those periods of time, you must not talk to any of the parties, their lawyers, or any of the witnesses.

If any attempt is made by anyone to talk to you concerning the matters here under consideration, you should immediately report that fact to the court.

You should keep an open mind. You should not form or express an opinion during the trial and should reach no conclusion in this case until you have heard all of the evidence, the arguments of counsel, and the final instructions as to the law, which will be given to you by the court.

1.02 CONDUCT OF THE TRIAL

First, the attorneys will have an opportunity to make opening statements. These statements are not evidence and should be considered only as a preview of what the attorneys expect the evidence will be.

Following opening statements, witnesses will be called to testify. They will be placed under oath and questioned by the attorneys. Documents and other tangible exhibits may also be received as evidence. If an exhibit is given to you to examine, you should examine it carefully, individually, and without any comment.

It is counsel's right and duty to object when testimony or other evidence is being offered that he or she believes is not admissible.

When the court sustains an objection to a question, you must disregard the question and the answer if one has been given, and draw no inference from the question or answer or speculate as to what the witness would have said if permitted to answer. You must also disregard evidence stricken from the record.

When the court sustains an objection to any evidence, you must disregard that evidence. When the court overrules an objection to any evidence, you must not give that evidence any more weight than if the objection had not been made.

When the evidence is completed, the attorneys will make final statements. These final statements are not evidence but are given to assist you in evaluating the evidence. The attorneys are also permitted to argue in an attempt to persuade you to a particular verdict. You may accept or reject those arguments as you see fit.

Finally, just before you retire to consider your verdict, I will give you further instructions on the law that applies to this case.

PART II.   FINAL INSTRUCTIONS

2.00   RESPECTIVE DUTIES OF JUDGE AND JURY

Ladies and gentlemen of the jury:

You have heard all the evidence and the arguments of the attorneys, and now it is my duty to instruct you on the law. You must arrive at your verdict by unanimous vote, applying the law, as you are now instructed, to the facts as you find them to be. The law applicable to this case is stated in these instructions, and it is your duty to follow all of them. You must not single out certain instructions and disregard others.

It is your duty to determine the facts, and to determine them only from the evidence in this case. You are to apply the law to the facts and in this way decide the case. You must not be governed or influenced by sympathy or prejudice for or against any party in this case.

Your verdict must be based on evidence and not upon speculation, guess or conjecture.

From time to time, the court has ruled on the admissibility of evidence. You must not concern yourselves with the reasons for these rulings. You should disregard questions and exhibits that were withdrawn or to which objections were sustained. You should also disregard testimony and exhibits that the court has refused or stricken. The evidence that you should consider consists only of the witnesses' testimony and the exhibits the court has received. Any evidence that was received for a limited purpose should not be considered by you for any other purpose. You should consider all the evidence in the light of your own observations and experiences in life.

Neither by these instructions nor by any ruling or remark that I have made do I mean to indicate any opinion as to the facts or as to what your verdict should be.

2.01   CREDIBILITY OF WITNESSES

You are the sole judges of the credibility of the witnesses and of the weight to be given to the testimony of each witness. In determining what credit is to be given any witness, you may take into account the witness's ability and opportunity to observe; the manner and appearance while testifying; any interest, bias, or prejudice the witness may have; the reasonableness of the testimony considered in the light of all the evidence; and any other factors that bear on the believability and weight of the witness's testimony.

2.02   DIRECT AND CIRCUMSTANTIAL EVIDENCE

The law recognizes two kinds of evidence: direct and circumstantial. Direct evidence proves a fact directly; that is, the evidence by itself, if true, establishes the fact. Circumstantial evidence is the proof of facts or circumstances that give rise to a reasonable inference of other facts; that is, circumstantial evidence proves a fact indirectly in that it follows from other facts or circumstances according to common experience and observations in life. An eyewitness is a common example of direct evidence, while human footprints are circumstantial evidence that a person was present.

The law makes no distinction between direct and circumstantial evidence as to the degree or amount of proof required, and each should be considered according to whatever weight or value it may have. All of the evidence should be considered and evaluated by you in arriving at your verdict.

2.03   "WILLFULLY"—DEFINED

The word "willfully," when applied to the intent with which an act is done or omitted, means with a purpose or willingness to commit the act or to make the omission in question. The word "willfully" does not require any intent to violate the law, or to injure another, or to acquire any advantage.

2.04   INFORMATION

The information in this case is the formal method of accusing the defendant of a crime and placing him on trial. It is not any evidence against the defendant and does not create any inference or guilt. The State has the burden of proving beyond a reasonable doubt every essential element of the crimes charged in the information.

2.05   PRESUMPTION OF INNOCENCE

The defendant is presumed to be innocent of the charges against him. This presumption remains with him throughout every stage of the trial and during your deliberations on the verdict. The presumption is not overcome until, from all the evidence in the case, you are convinced beyond a reasonable doubt that the defendant is guilty.

2.06   BURDEN OF PROOF

The State has the burden of proving the guilt of the defendant beyond a reasonable doubt, and this burden remains on the State throughout the case. The defendant is not required to prove his innocence.

2.07   REASONABLE DOUBT

Reasonable doubt means a doubt based upon reason and common sense that arises from a fair and rational consideration of all the evidence or lack of evidence in this case. It is a doubt that is not a vague, speculative, or imaginary doubt, but such a doubt as would cause reasonable persons to hesitate to act in matters of importance to themselves.

2.08   BELIEVABILITY OF A WITNESS—CONVICTION OF A CRIMINAL OFFENSE

The fact that a witness has been convicted of a criminal offense, if such be a fact, may be considered by you only for the purpose of determining the believability of that witness. The fact of such a conviction does not necessarily destroy or impair a witness's believability. It is one of the circumstances that you may take into consideration in weighing the testimony of such a witness.

2.09   MOTIVE

Motive is not an element of the crimes charged and need not be shown. However, you may consider motive or lack of motive as a circumstance in this case. Presence of motive may tend to establish guilt. Absence of motive may tend to establish innocence. You will therefore give its presence or absence, as the case may be, the weight to which you find it to be entitled.

2.10 DEFENDANT NOT TESTIFYING—NO INFERENCE OF GUILT MAY BE DRAWN

A defendant in a criminal trial has a constitutional right not to be compelled to testify. You must not draw any inference from the fact that a defendant does not testify. Further, you must neither discuss this matter nor permit it to enter into your deliberations in any way.

2.11 EXPERT TESTIMONY

A person is qualified to testify as an expert if [he] [she] has special knowledge, skill, experience, training, or education sufficient to qualify [him] [her] as an expert on the subject to which the testimony relates.

You are not bound to accept an expert opinion as conclusive, but should give to it the weight to which you find it to be entitled. You may disregard any such opinion if you find it to be unreasonable.

2.12 CHARGES

The State of Nita has charged the defendant, Darren Gray, with the crime of second-degree murder, which includes the crimes of voluntary manslaughter and criminally negligent homicide. If you are not satisfied beyond a reasonable doubt that the defendant is guilty of the crime charged, you may nevertheless convict the defendant of any lesser crime, if you are convinced beyond a reasonable doubt that the defendant is guilty of such lesser crime.

The defendant has pleaded not guilty.

2.13 SECOND-DEGREE MURDER

Under the Criminal Code of the State of Nita a person commits the crime of second-degree murder if:

1) He intentionally, but not after deliberation, causes the death of a person; or

2) With intent to cause serious injury to a person other than himself, he causes the death of that person or of another person.

A person acts intentionally with respect to a result or to conduct described by a statute defining a crime when his or her conscious objective is to cause such result or to engage in such conduct.

To sustain the charge of second-degree murder, the State must prove the following propositions:

1) That the defendant performed the acts which caused the death of Rudy York; and

2) That the defendant intended to kill or cause serious bodily injury to Rudy York.

If you find from your consideration of all the evidence that each of these propositions has been proven beyond a reasonable doubt, then you should find the defendant guilty of second-degree murder.

If, on the other hand, you find from your consideration of all the evidence that any of these propositions has not been proved beyond a reasonable doubt, then you should find the defendant not guilty of second-degree murder.

2.14   VOLUNTARY MANSLAUGHTER

Under the Criminal Code of the State of Nita, a person commits the crime of voluntary manslaughter if:

He intentionally, but not after deliberation, causes the death of a person under circumstances where the act causing the death was performed upon a sudden heat of passion caused by a serious and highly provoking act of the intended victim, affecting the person killing sufficiently to excite an irresistible passion in a reasonable person. However, if between the provocation and the killing there is an interval sufficient for the voice of reason and humanity to be heard, the killing is murder.

To sustain the charge of voluntary manslaughter, the State must prove that the defendant intentionally caused the death of Rudy York under circumstances where the act causing death was performed upon a sudden heat of passion caused by a serious and highly provoking act of the intended victim, Rudy York.

If you find from your consideration of all the evidence that this proposition has been proved beyond a reasonable doubt, then you should find the defendant guilty of voluntary manslaughter.

If, on the other hand, you find from your consideration of all the evidence that this proposition has not been proved beyond a reasonable doubt, then you should find the defendant not guilty of voluntary manslaughter.

2.15   CRIMINALLY NEGLIGENT HOMICIDE

Under the Criminal Code of the State of Nita a person commits the crime of criminally negligent homicide if:

1)   By conduct amounting to criminal negligence he causes the death of a person; or

2)   He intentionally causes the death of a person, but believes in good faith that circumstances exist which would justify his conduct, but that belief that such circumstances exist is unreasonable.

Conduct means an act or omission and its accompanying state of mind, or a series of acts or omissions.

A person acts with criminal negligence when, through a gross deviation from the standard of care that a reasonable person would exercise, he fails to perceive a substantial and unjustifiable risk that a result will occur or that a circumstance exists.

To sustain the charge of criminally negligent homicide the State must provide the following propositions:

1)   That the defendant performed the acts which caused the death of Rudy York, and

2)   That the defendant acted intentionally, but believed in good faith that circumstances existed which would have justified the killing of Rudy York, and his belief that such circumstances existed was unreasonable.

If you find from your consideration of all the evidence that each of these propositions has been proved beyond a reasonable doubt, then you should find the defendant guilty of criminally negligent homicide.

If, on the other hand, you find from your consideration of all the evidence that either of these propositions has not been proved beyond a reasonable doubt, then you should find the defendant not guilty of criminally negligent homicide.

2.16 SELF-DEFENSE

The defendant is not guilty of murder or voluntary manslaughter or criminally negligent homicide if he was justified in killing someone in self-defense. The defendant acted in lawful self-defense if:

1) The defendant reasonably believed that he was in imminent danger of being killed or suffering great bodily injury; *and*

2) The defendant reasonably believed that the immediate use of deadly force was necessary to defend against that danger; *and*

3) The defendant used no more force than was reasonably necessary to defend against that danger. Belief in future harm is not sufficient, no matter how great or how likely the harm is believed to be. The defendant must have believed there was imminent danger of death or great bodily injury to himself. The defendant's belief must have been reasonable, and he must have acted only because of that belief.

The defendant is only entitled to use that amount of force that a reasonable person would believe is necessary in the same situation. If the defendant used more force than was reasonable, the killing was not justified.

When deciding whether the defendant's beliefs were reasonable, consider all the circumstances as they were known to and appeared to the defendant, and consider what a reasonable person in a similar situation with similar knowledge would have believed. If the defendant's beliefs were reasonable, the danger does not need to have actually existed. The defendant's belief that he was threatened may be reasonable even if he relied on information that was not true. However, the defendant must actually and reasonably have believed that the information was true.

A defendant is not required to retreat. He is entitled to stand his ground and defend himself and, if reasonably necessary, to pursue an assailant until the danger of death or great bodily injury has passed. This is so even if safety could have been achieved by retreating.

Great bodily injury means significant or substantial physical injury. It is an injury that is greater than minor or moderate harm.

The State has the burden of proving beyond a reasonable doubt that the killing was not justified. If the State has not met this burden, you must find the defendant not guilty of murder or voluntary manslaughter or criminally negligent homicide.

2.17 RIGHT TO SELF DEFENSE: MUTUAL COMBAT OR INITIAL AGGRESSOR

A person who engages in mutual combat or who starts a fight has a right to self-defense only if:

1) He actually and in good faith tried to stop fighting; *and*

2) He indicated, by word or by conduct, to his opponent, in a way that a reasonable person would understand, that he wanted to stop fighting and that he had stopped fighting; *and*

3) He gave his opponent a chance to stop fighting. If the defendant meets these requirements, he then had a right to self-defense if the opponent continued to fight. [However, if the defendant used only non-deadly force, and the opponent responded with such sudden and deadly force that the defendant could not withdraw from the fight, then the defendant

had the right to defend himself with deadly force and was not required to try to stop fighting, communicate the desire to stop to the opponent, or give the opponent a chance to stop fighting.]

A fight is *mutual combat* when it began or continued by mutual consent or agreement. That agreement may be expressly stated or implied and must occur before the claim to self-defense arose.

2.18   MISTAKE OF FACT

You have heard evidence that the defendant's actions were based on a mistake of fact. Mistake of fact is a defense. You are required to find the defendant not guilty if:

1)   The defendant actually believed that Rudy York had a weapon;

2)   The defendant's belief and actions were reasonable under the circumstances; *or*

3)   The defendant did not intend to commit the crimes of murder of the second degree or voluntary manslaughter or criminally negligent homicide and the defendant's conduct would not have amounted to any one of those crimes if the mistaken belief had been correct, meaning that, if the true facts were what the defendant thought them to be, the defendant's conduct would not have been criminal.

In order to convict the defendant, the State must prove beyond a reasonable doubt that at least one of the three factors was absent.

2.19   JUSTIFIABLE HOMICIDE BY PUBLIC OFFICER

The defendant is not guilty of murder or voluntary manslaughter or criminally negligent homicide if he killed someone while acting as a public officer. Such a killing is justified and therefore not unlawful if:

1)   The defendant was a public officer;

2)   The killing was committed while overcoming actual resistance to some legal process or while performing any a legal duty;

3)   The killing was necessary to accomplish one of those lawful purposes; *and*

4)   The defendant had probable cause to believe that Rudy York posed a threat of death or great bodily injury, either to the defendant or to others, and that crime threatened the defendant or others with death or great bodily injury.

Deadly force may not be used to prevent the escape of an apparently unarmed suspected felon unless it is necessary to prevent the escape and the officer has probable cause to believe that the suspect poses a significant threat of death or serious physical injury to the officer or others.

A person has *probable cause* to believe that someone poses a significant threat of death or great bodily injury when facts known to the person would persuade someone of reasonable caution that the other person is going to cause death or great bodily injury to another.

An officer or employee of the Nita City Police Department is a *public officer*.

Great bodily injury means significant or substantial physical injury. It is an injury that is greater than minor or moderate harm.

Where the accused is a public officer, the reasonableness of the conduct must be evaluated not from the perspective of a reasonable civilian but rather from the perspective of a reasonable public officer similarly situated.

The State has the burden of proving beyond a reasonable doubt that the killing was not justified. If the State has not met this burden, you must find the defendant not guilty of murder or voluntary manslaughter or criminally negligent homicide.

2.20   JURY MUST NOT CONSIDER PENALTY

In your deliberations, do not discuss or consider the subject of penalty or punishment. That subject must not in any way affect your verdict.

2.21   CONCLUDING INSTRUCTION

You shall now retire and select one of your number to act as presiding juror. He or she will preside over your deliberations. In order to reach a verdict, all jurors must agree to the decision. As soon as all of you have agreed upon a verdict, so that each may state truthfully that the verdict expresses his or her vote, have it dated and signed by your presiding juror and return with it to the courtroom.

THE STATE OF NITA	)	
	)	Case No. CR 3914-YR-1
v.	)	
	)	JURY VERDICT
DARREN GRAY,	)	
Defendant.	)	

We, the jury, return the following verdict, and each of us concurs in this verdict:

[Choose the appropriate verdict]

I. <u>NOT GUILTY</u>

We, the jury, find the defendant, Darren Gray, NOT GUILTY.

_____

Presiding Juror

II. <u>GUILTY</u>

We, the jury, find the defendant, Darren Gray, GUILTY of the crime of:

_____ Murder in the Second Degree

_____ Voluntary Manslaughter

_____ Criminally Negligent Homicide

_____

Presiding Juror

Made in United States
Orlando, FL
16 January 2024

42568236R00089